Forsaken are the Peacemakers

by

Michael J. Reidy

Dorrance Publishing Co
Alpha Drive
Pittsburgh, PA 15238
Visit our website at www.dorrancebookstore.com

ISBN: 979-8-8852-7424-1
eISBN: 979-8-8860-4906-0

To the men who helped me along the way:
Ralph Gallagher, Esq.;
John Bustamante, Esq.;
George Lemmerman;
and Joe Kostal,
the best Boy Scout Troop Leader there ever was.

Also, my thanks to John Soat and Victoria Dixon
for their input and assistance.

Book I

Alexander Chastain

The descendent of Polish immigrants, United States Senator Alexander Chastain was tall, at six foot one, and very attractive. The blond hair from his mother's side was Robert Redford-like and always expensively shorn. He had a patrician nose, deep blue eyes, and was a fanatic about staying fit. His frame was built for expensive suits; he could have been a model. Many women were fascinated by him, almost as if he were some kind of rock star. After the family business was sold for millions and his father retired from the bench, Alexander and his family relocated permanently to their Florida compound. At age 32 he was appointed to an open congressional seat there, and at 42, he became Florida's junior senator. Now 46, he was, perhaps, on the doorstep of the presidency. Though he had made no formal announcement, Chastain had already begun his quest for his party's nomination.

Chastain was scheduled to appear on The Sunday Morning Roundtable to be interviewed by Carson Nelson, one of the network's most popular talking heads. A few days prior to the interview, a photo had come to light of three American soldiers in full gear urinating on the bodies of Iraqi insurgents they had just killed. In less than a day, the photograph had gone viral, travelling around the globe via the internet. Chastain couldn't have imagined a better stage or time to promote his candidacy and his agenda on foreign affairs. He believed the American people were fed up, they wanted a fresh voice and a new way of looking at things. They needed to understand America's "new" unenviable position in the court of public opinion, dictated in large part by the American downing of Iran Air Flight 655; the abuses at Abu Ghraib; water boarding at Guantanamo; the gang-rape and murder of 14-year-old Abeer Qasim Hamza, and the effort to cover it up by the murder of her entire family; and now this vile desecration of fallen Iraqis. True, the dead were insurgents; however, they were still men, and they were being pissed on by these Americans with smiles on their faces. Chastain knew most Iraqis believed their country had been pissed on by America for years. The billions of dollars America was spending overseas reaped only hatred for the country. Most Americans, however, failed to understand why and were fed up. Chastain believed he could ride their discontent to the nomination and, perhaps, all the way to the presidency.

On the Sunday morning Chastain was to be interviewed, the network studio was abuzz, especially the women. Everyone came to work early that Sunday, and some even came in despite being off. Each hoped for an opportunity to see the "rock star" senator from Florida close up, and perhaps get a chance to speak with him.

When he arrived, he was immediately met by the station bigwigs and then guided to the small makeup room where he quickly identified the "target." The young, shapely cosmetologist was a blonde named Sherry and she could not hide her blush when Chastain was guided to her chair. He took her hand and felt the tremble. The other women looking on wanted to kill her, they were so envious. Even though she had known for weeks the task of preparing Chastain for the TV cameras was hers, she was still unprepared for the feelings rising within her. He immediately recognized Sherry was going to be an easy mark.

"So, Sherry, how long have you worked here?"

"Uh going on three years, Senator."

"Don't be so nervous."

"You have no idea, Senator."

"Well, I hope it's nothing I did and, please, why don't you just call me Alex?"

With a chuckle, "I don't think so."

"I'm calling you Sherry, so you just call me Alex and we'll get along fine. Perhaps when I'm done here, I can introduce you to some of the campaign staff. After the interview, we are going to have a little brunch over at the hotel and you are certainly welcome to come along. Would you like that?"

"Gee, I don't know, maybe. Well, I guess that would be alright."

"Sure it is. I'll just tell your boss that you are going to get the 'inside scoop' on what it's like to be on the campaign trail. He'll appreciate that."

Sherry was blushing again.

Rising from the chair, Chastain winked at his bodyguard and nodded toward Sherry. The bodyguard approached her immediately and told her he would escort her back to the hotel following the television interview. He knew the drill; he had done it more times than he could count.

It wasn't five minutes into the television interview before Nelson began the discussion of Chastain's stance on foreign affairs and the stage was set.

"Carson, don't misunderstand me. I believe the United States is the greatest country in the history of the world. But in foreign affairs we have lost our way and many of our world neighbors now hold us in contempt. Representatives from both political parties wrongly believe the 9/11 hijackers did what they did because of their envy for us. Carson, that is not true. They did what they did because of our country's failed diplomacy in the region...which has lasted for decades. The 9/11 hijackers wanted nothing more from us than to be left alone. They wanted us to stop meddling in their affairs.

"When will we abandon our Don Quixote quest to impose democracy in the Middle East? When we finally realize the strict religious beliefs, mores, and traditions of these countries will not allow it. The people of the Middle East fail to see the virtue in democracy and who can blame them? They only see abuse at the hands of Americans: Abu Ghraib, Guantanamo, waterboarding, the rape and murder of civilians by American soldiers, American drones killing innocent people, and this latest desecration of their dead. In a democracy, it is acceptable to desecrate bodies by urinating on them? If this is democracy at work, would any of us want it? The American public has no concept for the upheaval America has caused."

In a rather gruff manner, Nelson replied, "Senator Chastain, I certainly understand mistakes have been made by some of our wayward military but those are isolated incidents. What do you mean when you say we meddle in their affairs?"

"Carson, we need to look at America through the eyes of others. And not just in the Middle East, either. Humor me for a moment and close your eyes."

Nelson scoffed at Chastain's request.

"No, seriously, close your eyes." Looking straight into the camera Chastain said, "You folks at home do the same. Close your eyes and imagine you are driving along the California coast. Can you do that, Carson?"

With a smirk, "Okay. I'll play along."

"Good. Okay, now picture this. You are in a convertible with the top down. You are driving along a California highway headed north. It is a beautiful summer day and it's 80 degrees outside. To your left you see the majestic Pacific lapping up against white sand beaches. You then look to the east and you see breathtaking snowcapped mountain ranges in the far distance highlighted by the noon sun. As you go along the road, it turns away from the coast and takes you a bit inland to the east. Along that stretch of road, you begin to see large yellow signs with bold black lettering that say, "RESTRICTED AREA. DO NOT LEAVE YOUR AUTOMOBILE." You realize you are fast approaching an air force base and you see and hear fighter jets overhead. Can you imagine all that?"

"Yes, but I guess my question would be, so what?"

"You don't mind the detour in the road, the air force base, or the noise of the jets because they give you a sense of security and, perhaps, even pride. Would you agree with me on that?"

"Yes."

"Okay fine. Now imagine it's a Chinese Air Force base."

"A Chinese Air Force base in California!?"

"It is home to fifty-five hundred Chinese nationals and the jets overhead are being flown by Chinese fighter pilots. What do you think now?"

"That will never happen."

"You didn't answer the question. I asked you to imagine it was a Chinese air base and I asked you how that would make you feel."

"It would scare the hell out of me."

"That's what I thought. Now realize the United States currently maintains 190 military bases on foreign soil."

Silence.

"Carson?"

Silence.

"Carson, I'll tell you what. Here's another example. The greatest country in the history of the world, the United States, has a nuclear arsenal that can destroy the entire planet. Its air force and submarine fleet possess the ability to deliver a nuclear warhead to the four corners of the globe and your country is absolutely powerless to stop it. Your country is in a volatile region and has antagonists on two of its borders and it, too, is developing a nuclear capability. The United States wants to keep membership in the nuclear "club" to the select few and, obviously, that does not include you. The U.S. threatens your country with economic sanctions and even military action should you continue in your efforts to develop a nuclear capability. How is it the United States has the right to impose its will on your country? Whether your development of a nuclear weapon is a good thing or a bad thing, what gives the United States, or any other country for that matter, the right to say you cannot do it? What gives us the right to threaten your country because you are trying to accomplish what we accomplished decades ago?"

"Senator, I don't believe we would initiate such heavy-handed diplomacy as you describe. I believe we would open a dialogue with such a country. I can only hope, senator, you do not believe the proliferation of nuclear weapons is a good thing." Nelson clearly thought he had one-upped the young Florida lawmaker.

"Certainly, I agree with you. But what you're saying is we would engage in discussions with such a country and ask them to forgo their own nuclear capability because they can trust us. We will be the gatekeeper, the protector of the globe. There is no need for more nuclear armament because we have everything under control. Isn't that what you're saying?"

"Yes."

"Okay then, will you answer one last question for me?"

"I'll try my best."

"What country is the only one in the history of the world to unleash a nuclear holocaust, not upon a military target but upon a city?"

Silence.

"Carson?"

Silence.

"And once wasn't enough, was it?"

No answer.

"How trusting would you be?"

Silence.

"Carson, before we leave the subject of foreign policy, let me say this. I have been labeled many things by many different people, but I am neither a 'dove' nor am I an 'isolationist.' I believe in developing state-of-the-art weapons and maintaining a strong military to protect our shores. I simply believe such force should be dedicated to the protection of our great country and should not be used to interfere in the affairs of others regardless of how we may abhor their politics. I also believe we should engage in humanitarian efforts whenever possible, but when it comes down to military intervention, we have an institution called the United Nations. If anything more than our humanitarian effort is called for, it should be through that institution. The United States should never have become and can no longer be the 'policeman of the world.' In terms of American lives and, yes, American money, we can no longer afford it. The loss of over 58,000 American lives in Vietnam taught us nothing. Who was it who said, 'If we do not study our history, we will be condemned to repeat it?"

Alexander Chastain had thrived at college and excelled at law school. His debate skills were well honed and his ability to communicate on all levels might just get him the nomination. His public persona, much different from the true lecherous Alexander, was something a voter could buy into. Right now, though, Chastain was growing tired of the rhetoric. He was distracted, thinking about what's-her-name he just met.

The Burks

"So now, what do you think?" Carrie Burk asked her husband, Bobby Lee, who was lying in the bed next to the beautiful wife he adored. He was only half-listening to Chastain's Sunday morning interview.

Months ago, the Burks had stopped attending Sunday services. Carrie's prayers had gone unanswered, so she stopped praying. Almost every week, she read newspaper accounts of child abuse and neglect by those who had been blessed with children...so why was she denied? The first Sunday morning they skipped church, Carrie spent clearing out the nursery, which had been sitting idle for the better part of two years awaiting their firstborn. She sold everything the following week at her garage sale, and the next four months were spent in such a deep depression she needed professional counseling.

When Bobby Lee had returned from his duty in the first Iraqi encounter, Operation Desert Storm, he had opened his gun shop in Carrie's hometown of Crawford. Now, years later, they were making a decent living. Carrie helped with the bookwork on the weekends, but during the week, she preferred to work in her girlfriend's daycare for children. The Burks didn't really need the extra money. The work was more therapeutic for Carrie than anything else.

Bobby Lee didn't like Alexander Chastain. Burk had risked his life in Iraq and he didn't need some silver-spooned politician telling him his friends died in vain. Bobby was truly a "self-made man," whereas Chastain was born on third base but went through life trying to convince others he had hit a triple. The tragic irony lost on most Americans was politicians like Chastain held the power to send courageous men like Burk into one hell or another, often to their deaths. The closest thing Chastain came to the sands of Iraq, Bobby Lee knew, was the resort beaches of South Florida and the bikinis he chased.

"He doesn't know what he is talking about."

"Well, it seems to make sense to me."

"Doesn't it bother you this guy never worked a day in his life and never came remotely close to military service?"

Truth be told, like many other women, Carrie was enamored with the incredibly attractive and eloquent senator from Florida. "I was thinking of volunteering on his campaign."

"You're kidding."

"Why? I like his message."

"He is just saying what needs to be said so he can get elected. He has no experience in foreign affairs."

"You have to agree what he says makes a lot of sense."

"I think what he says ignores reality. Chastain may have forgotten how Japan forced us into the war. Carrie, tens of thousands of American lives would have been lost in the invasion of Japan had it not been for Hiroshima and Nagasaki. People were going to die; our military leaders just decided it would be their people and not ours. Also, had America not stepped up to become 'the policeman of the world,' we would all be speaking either German or Russian right now. There was no one else strong enough to face the tyrants. The United Nations is an admirable concept, but that's all it is—a concept. It still does not work, even after all these years."

"I understand he's coming to Cleveland for a rally, and Eileen and I thought we might go there to see him."

"Suit yourself. Right now, I'm just interested in getting those pajamas off you so I can get to that luscious body of yours."

"No way."

"I tell you what—you can pretend I'm a senator."

"Oh, okay then."

As he pulled her top over her head and exposed those incredible firm breasts, he laughed and said, "You are rotten."

She laughingly replied, "Anything you say...senator."

Bobby Lee was also incredibly saddened by their failure to have children; however, he was secretly happy her beautiful body was not ravaged by the stretch marks or excess weight brought on by childbirth. She was exactly the same as she was at age nineteen when they had sex for the first time. Her blonde hair caressed her face, her arms and legs were long and angular, her waist was small and she had the cutest tush a man could ask for. She was a "head-turner."

Unlike his beautiful wife, Bobby Lee had lost his idealism long ago, if he ever had any. Growing up in backward Rehoboth outside of New Lexington, you only had one goal as a young man and that was to leave there as soon as you could. You didn't have time to be idealistic about anything. Since the only way out for a poor young kid was military service, Bobby Lee joined up after graduation, left his home and never returned. In the service, he learned about weaponry, lost whatever idealism he may have had in the worthless sands of Iraq, and then was fortunate to meet his beautiful Carrie. Military service helped transform a naive country-bumpkin kid from southeast Ohio into a brave young man, devoted husband, and ultimately, a successful business owner. No one could blow smoke up Bobby Lee Burk's ass.

Ted Chase

Crawford attorney Ted Chase also made it a point to watch the Sunday morning interview. He and his wife, Dorie, were spending a weekend alone at his in-laws' cottage up at the lake while the kids were being watched by Mom and Dad back home. Dorie was still asleep as he diced the ingredients for the omelet and listened to the small television that sat on the wide corner windowsill of the kitchen. As soon as he saw the close-up of the senator with his incredibly good looks and blonde locks, Ted began to understand all the commotion.

"Carson, before we leave the subject of foreign policy, let me say this. I have been labeled many things by many different people, but I am neither a 'dove' nor am I an 'isolationist.'"

Ted thought the guy was brilliant. He had come up with an almost unassailable position that, given the current climate in America, would probably get him the nomination. Americans were fed up with the situation in the Middle East, fed up with seeing young Americans die there for no good reason, fed up with seeing their retirement funds sacrificed to taxes to support the military effort there. They were fed up with reports of Saudi sheiks, supported by the United States, obscenely squandering millions; ignoring what rights their citizens had; and treating women worse than chattel. But Ted knew there was much more to the story than Chastain was sharing. Chastain was only doing what every politician before him had done: He was spouting what the electorate wanted to hear, but he was offering no solutions. The Middle East had long been, and continued to be, the world's powder keg about to explode at any minute.

"The United Nations? You've got to be kidding," Ted muttered to himself. It was right then that Dorie shuffled into the kitchen wearing her footy pajamas and scratching her backside.

"Who are you talking to?"

"No one. Just myself."

"You know, it's when you start answering yourself that you may have a real problem," she chuckled a bit. "What do you have on the set?"

"I was watching this interview with this Chastain character."

"He's a cutie, isn't he?"

"Yeah, he's not bad looking. He seems to have a lot to say but doesn't really seem to be offering any solutions. He just offered the United Nations as a solution to the mess in the Middle East. That tells me he doesn't really have a grasp on the entire situation. But he has a very popular message."

"I don't think anyone has an answer to that mess. He probably would do no worse than past administrations."

"You may be right, but it's time someone comes forward with something constructive. Otherwise, it will just be more of the same."

"He's going to get the female vote, you can count on that."

"That's a little shallow, don't you think?"

"Maybe."

Ted picked up the cutting board, angled it toward the pan with the melting butter, and with a brush of the knife dumped the diced onions, peppers, and tomatoes into the pan. They started to sizzle and fill the small kitchen with their pleasant aroma. Dorie put two slices of potato bread in the toaster then poured two cups of black coffee. She pressed her breasts into Ted's back and placed her arms around his waist as he sautéed the vegetables. She only came up to about the middle of his shoulder blades. He turned and kissed her on the forehead. When he finished creating the huge omelet, he cut it in half, slid each half on a plate, turned off the set and sat down with Dorie at the kitchen table.

"This is terrific," Dorie said with a mouthful.

"What did you expect?"

"I think I may keep you just a little longer."

"That's comforting to hear. You know, this is going to cost you."

"Really? What did you have in mind?"

Ted was the managing attorney of Rosenthall & Chase Co., LPA, a four-partner general practice firm in small, rural Crawford, Ohio. The firm, which had been in existence all of three years, began as an office-sharing arrangement between litigator Ted Chase and real estate specialist Jay Rosenthall. When Ted had grown disenchanted with the inequities of his former firm and chose to strike out on his own, Jay, a sole practitioner, cut Ted a sweetheart deal to share office space. Soon after Ted opened his practice, two other "refugees" from Ted's former firm, Larry Tehan and Greg Rothgery, came knocking. Tehan was a corporate attorney and Rothgery specialized in wills and trusts; both had substantial books of business. It was decided the four lawyers would create a new partnership and the firm was born. Ted's retired trial practice professor from law school, James McIlvaine, reverently referred to as "Mac," was added "of counsel." Shortly after Rosenthall Chase set up shop, two "high-profile" cases had come Ted's way, providing the best publicity for the new firm (the free kind), and conferring upon it instant status within the county's small legal community. Unlike the firm Ted had left, this new partnership was financially prudent and fair, creating a healthy, workable balance between income generation and family life. Ted and Dorie Chase were happily married for almost twenty years and were the parents of three children, two girls and a boy. The only other members of Ted's family included his seventy-two-year-old mother and his older sister Elizabeth, who lived with her. Ted was six feet tall with sharp features, deep blue eyes, and a full head of black/gray pepper hair. He was still in pretty good shape, only ten pounds or so over his college weight. Dorie was a good half foot shorter than Ted and, she, too, kept herself in good shape. She continued to go to the rec center three times a week. She had curly dishwater blonde hair, brown eyes, a turned-up nose, and high cheeks.

Growing up, Ted was very close to his older sister and many of the events in her life also shaped Ted's. They both recognized Lizzie was favored by their father but, realizing this, she did nothing to press her advantage. Ted flourished, in part, because of her understanding and deep love for her little brother. He was very successful: scholarship to college, Rhodes Scholar nominee, captain of the baseball team, Law Review, top ten percent in his law school class, successful litigator, and now, managing partner of his own law firm.

The fact that his sister had chosen nursing for a career and wanted to focus on pediatrics surprised no one, especially Ted. He was really her first patient, as she doted for years on her little brother. She was accepted by several nursing schools including the one out of state in Eau Claire specializing in pediatrics and was awarded both grants and scholarships. It was the most natural extension of her life: She was going to become a nurse to children facing disease and medical treatments that scared them sometimes even worse than their disease. Because of her little brother Ted, she possessed the tools for her trade before she took one hour of nursing classes.

But a tragic event in her life would further shape Ted's. Ted would never forget the call or the sight of his father slumped at the kitchen table weeping bitterly, Ted's mother standing at his side holding the telephone. He had never seen his father cry and it scared him. The dean of students at the nursing school Lizzie attended hundreds of miles away was informing his father she had been admitted to the hospital, a victim of what was reported to be a date rape.

What eventually killed Ted's father was not only his failure to protect his sweet daughter; it was his inability to avenge her. The bastard they never arrested came from a wealthy, high-profile family with "connections" throughout the State. The matter was never prosecuted; it was swept under the rug. The media was somehow silenced. Not a word got out. Ted's parents knew what happened but the boy and his family, long-time benefactors of the school, remained protected. When, after days of asking, Ted's parents finally got the chance to talk with the local prosecutor, his agenda was crystal clear. He spoke of "consensual sex" and talked about what he could or could not prove. Such excuses successfully sheltered the rich son-of-a-bitch from "these Chase people from Ohio" and quashed any thoughts of a criminal prosecution. Nothing came of it. But Elizabeth would never be the same and her father would eventually wither and die because of what another man did to his precious daughter. Ted's hope was that someday someone would nail the prick, and he looked forward to when he would read the account of the son-of-a-bitch going down. But it never came. In fact, just the opposite occurred; the bastard flourished. Truth be told, Elizabeth's tragedy was one of the reasons Ted sought a career in the law, and the events in her life continued to shape Ted's.

Elizabeth didn't flourish. His sister could only be described as withdrawn and reclusive. She left school after the incident and went on to accomplish nothing in her life. She never graduated, she had no family of her own, no job, and no prospects...nothing. At age forty-seven, she still lived with her widowed mother.

Tony Icovatti

"Sal, you gotta' come over here and listen to this shit."

"No way. Waste of time. Besides, I got the winner."

Chastain's interview had made it halfway across the world to the army barracks within the Green Zone of Baghdad where Army Ranger Corporal Anthony Icovatti, sometimes called Tony, but more often referred to as just "T," was intently watching while his best friend Salvatore Colonna waited to play ping pong.

"Sally, you're a moron."

"Yeah, I know. But tell me who the moron is who talked me into joining up and getting sent to this fuckin' place."

Got a point there, T thought to himself. But 39 more days and their unit was going home. "According to this asshole, this whole thing was a huge mistake."

"He's right."

"He doesn't know what he is talking about."

The relationship between Salvatore Colonna and Tony Icovatti started off with a school yard fight on the playground of St. Rocco's. T started it because he was calling Salvatore "Sally." As they were waiting for Sister Joachim to decide their fate, they began to realize they had quite a bit in common. In a short time, they became friends. Two months later, they were in Sister Joachim's office once again for fighting. This time, T had come to Sally's aid as he was being taunted by some of the older kids. Though they were younger and outnumbered, Sally and T beat hell out of Sally's tormentors, and from that point forward, they were inseparable. Between the two of them, Salvatore's nickname stuck, but T was the only person on the planet who was allowed to use it. The older kids learned to leave them alone. They knew if they went after Salvatore, they would have to answer to T.

The boys were only fifteen years old on September 11, 2001 when they sat together and watched innocent people fling themselves from the roofs of the Twin Towers just before they collapsed. Sally did not understand why but T explained it to him.

"Sally, they don't want to burn to death. They are making a choice." His parents did not know it, but T also made a choice that day as they watched the Towers implode...and he shared his decision with Sally.

Both were outstanding high school athletes. On the football team, they were the star tandem defensive backs. On the baseball team, Sally was the pitcher and T was his catcher. They were inseparable both on and off the playing fields. They always knew where each other was and never thought about doing anything without first consulting the other. When they were juniors, they dated the Cusummano twins; it was almost as if they were going out with the same girl. The Icovattis considered Sally to be their sixth child and the Colonnas felt the same way about T. It would have been unusual for the Colonnas to take a vacation without including T and the same could be said for the Icovattis and Sally. Their parents became fast friends who oftentimes kidded the boys about their relationship, but truth be told, they admired them for it. Many people who came to know the boys would say they were as close as brothers, but they would be wrong; they were much closer.

Both T and Sally had a picture on their bedroom walls of Pat Tillman in his number forty Arizona Cardinals uniform. Neither set of parents thought it unusual for a high school football player to have a poster of their favorite NFL player on their wall. The fact these two boys liked the same player, also a defensive back, certainly came as no surprise to anyone. However, their parents didn't know the whole story; they saw only a football player. T and Sally saw an incredibly brave and patriotic young man who chucked a career in the NFL and a $3.6 million-dollar salary so that, after 9/11, he could enlist in the Army and become a Ranger like his brother who was also a gifted athlete. Tillman served in the same unit as his brother in Operation Mountain Storm in Afghanistan where he made the ultimate sacrifice. T went to work to convince his best friend that they, too, were going to become Rangers. They were going to go off to war together, but unlike Tillman, they were going to triumphantly return to their small town as heroes; that was their plan.

With the exception of T's older brother who went to work on the family farm, all the children in the two families continued their educations and both sets of parents expected the boys to do the same. Without their parents' knowledge, however, the boys had already met with a recruiter to gather information about the financial aid programs offered by the Army. They had to present enlistment to their parents as something positive, simply a first step toward the ultimate goal of a college diploma. They calculated that this approach would soften the blow, especially to their mothers.

Vice President Harley Daull

"This son-of-a-bitch is going to be a real problem for us," said Harley Daull after he clicked off the television and looked at his confidant and "go-to guy," Chester Mylott. "I've been living in the shadow of an idiot President for seven fuckin' years and now this pecker-head is stirring everything up and getting in the way. United Nations, are you kidding me? What are the polls saying?"

"It's really much too early to tell, Harley."

"Have you spoken to the Chairman recently?"

"The party isn't going to make any commitments this early in the primary."

Vice President Harley Daull was concerned, and with good reason. He never got along with the Chairman of the Democratic Party, and he fully understood and appreciated what he just witnessed on television. He had been planning his run for the nation's highest office for the last three years, assuming all along he would be his party's nominee. Chastain's performance on national television that morning changed everything.

Harley Daull's family owned the largest dairy farm in Wisconsin. His power base was the State's Farm Bureau, which had been led by his millionaire father for the better part of twenty years. At an early age, Daull had witnessed political wheeling and dealing close up and he had learned well. As he followed in his father's footsteps, he realized the value of his father's advice: "It's not what you are that is important. It's what the people think you are." Well "the people" eventually came to know Harley Daull as a hardworking farm boy who was the champion of the "little guy" and they eventually elected him their governor. In reality, Daull was another version of Alexander Chastain, just without the charm and good looks.

Now age fifty-two, Daull was a rather large man at six foot four with thinning hair and jowly cheeks. His facial features were rather "thick," especially his nose and ears. He was a bit paunchy in the gut and always appeared somewhat uncomfortable in a suit. He would never grace the cover of Gentleman's Quarterly.

Seven years ago, after so-so showings in several presidential primaries, he became the compromise pick for Vice President. The presidential nominee was a two-term senator from New York, and he needed Daull to appease those party members who wanted a Washington "outsider" to round out the ticket, preferably someone with Midwestern roots. The party promised Daull a proactive role as Vice President to entice him to run, but the President-elect neither liked nor appreciated him. Daull was perceived by the East Coast intellectuals and Washington insiders who dominated the new Cabinet as not bright. "Dull Daull" they would call him.

During the two terms of his vice-presidency, Daull had no access to a President who needed him to get elected, but never respected him. Seven long years, Daull was stranded on an island within the administration, and for seven long years, he bristled. The only time he entered the Oval Office was when he was summoned to be assigned yet another meaningless task, and even that was often done by a subordinate.

About two years ago, it was actually a White House intern who conveyed to Daull what the President wanted. And it was then Daull began to consider "Plan B." He had grown to hate the New York son-of-a-bitch and his East Coast cronies who mocked him, but even so, Daull was "only a heartbeat away from the presidency." If that heart were to stop beating. At the time, Daull had confided with the only man he could trust, Chester Mylott.

Every professional politician needs a "corner man," a confidant who could deftly move "behind the scenes," make contacts and cut deals while ensuring his boss maintained 100% deniability, a man trusted to handle the most sensitive task without leaving "fingerprints." Chester Mylott was such a man. Early on, a young, naive Mylott acted out of his belief in Daull and his political agenda. But as Mylott grew older, his idealism wore off—a casualty of political reality. Now in his late forties, Mylott's goal was much simpler: just stick around long enough to make enough money so he wouldn't need this crap any longer. He had never married so he was not far from his goal. Another four years would just about do it. Another eight, for sure.

When Daull's hatred of the President had reached a crescendo and he suggested "Plan B" to Mylott, Chester had actually made a call or two...but, eventually, common sense prevailed. They wisely reconsidered and decided to await the next election when Daull would certainly be anointed the standard bearer for the Democratic Party. That day was finally here, but so was Alexander Chastain.

"What do we have on Chastain?"

"Not much, but we've got someone working on it."

"Who?"

"Patronite."

"Patronite? Is he any good?"

"He's a she, and yes, she's good."

"We have a woman on Chastain?"

"Harley, given what we suspect about Chastain, we decided a female was the way to go. Patronite is sharp. If there is something out there, she will find it. Believe me, I know. I have the marks to show for it."

"Pull back on the others."

"You're serious?"

"Yes. This is the guy we will have to beat. The others don't stand a chance. No sense spending the money." Secretly, Daull now worried if he had a chance.

"You sure?" Mylott could sense his boss's fear.

"Yes! How long has Patronite been on it?"

"Couple 'o weeks."

"Find out what she knows."

"Harley, it's only been two weeks."

"I don't give a shit! Once a snowball starts rolling downhill, it becomes a fuckin' avalanche. She needs to understand that. We need to get the dirt on this asshole now! Hell, everyone knows he can't keep it in his pants! What's the problem? I want to know if she has anything."

"I'll call her tomorrow morning."

Marie Patronite

Marie Patronite was the best of the best. She had all the tools: fierce drive, solid instincts, incredible intelligence and...she had a lot of contacts and knew all the "players." The fact that she was attractive, with flowing blonde hair and a noteworthy figure didn't hurt either.

Politics was in her blood. She was the daughter of the late senior senator from Connecticut but few knew because she kept her married name after her divorce. Frankly, she despised her father and was glad to be rid of his name. She was an Ivy League law school graduate who had worked on many campaigns and for both parties—whoever got to her first and could pay her fee. Her only allegiance was to her 401K.

Mylott's first encounter with her was adversarial. His candidate had not been entirely candid...and when he went down in flames thanks to Patronite's "research," Mylott promised himself it would never happen again, and he made sure by getting to her first.

When she took Mylott's call two weeks ago, Patronite was excited and immediately accepted. She was now on the biggest stage imaginable and...she could probably double her usual fee. If there were any dirt on Alexander Chastain, Patronite would uncover it. Patronite knew national politics in America had been going down the sewer since Gary Hart took his ill-fated boat ride. It was becoming an increasingly dirty business and she had made it into a lucrative one.

"Marie, this is Chester Mylott. Daull wants to know what we have on Chastain."

"Not much yet...family history. Scholastic career that appears to be legit...took all his own law school examinations...and did well, by the way, Order of the Coif. Has yet to drive off a bridge with a girl in the backseat..."

"Very funny."

"Look, I'm just getting started here."

"I know, but Chastain has got Daull spooked. We need to crank this up. He actually called off the dogs on the other candidates."

"Really? A bit premature, wouldn't you say?"

"I think so. An awful lot can happen in the next fifteen months but it's not my call. He's convinced Chastain is the guy. Have you got anything good?"

"Nothing more than the rumors everyone has already heard."

"Well, ramp it up if you can and let me know when you have anything, will you? Anything at all."

"Will do."

Marie's entry into the world of politics was because of her mother, the Connecticut senator's first wife, who now resided in a private facility on Long Island—the wife he neglected. Her mother sacrificed herself to the role: the dutiful, devoted spouse of an entrenched three-term senator...while she slowly died on the inside. A young Marie watched it all come about. The rumors of her father's infidelities ultimately engulfed her mother and took her mind. When the bastard died two trophy wives later, Marie shed no tears, nor did her mother. Death, like many other things, was something her mother could no longer comprehend.

Marie understood her parents were throwbacks to an earlier era, a time when the infidelity of powerful men was seemingly expected but never exposed. Now, as she drove back to the city from a visit with her mother, her eyes teared as Marie felt some measure of guilt... but inappropriately so. After all, at the time, Marie was much too young to do anything while she, too, was being neglected by her father. The only thing Marie could do now was visit with her mother as often as possible, bring her small gifts, talk with her, read to her and comb her gray hair.

Marie did not realize it, but her father left indelible marks on her as well. Trust of anyone, men in particular, did not come easily to her. Her fourteen-month relationship with handsome Nicholas, a classmate at Cornell, was a marathon by her standards, but was mutually ended. She was now alone and happier that way, consumed by her work. The country was at a turning point, and she was retained by the Vice President for what could be the biggest political battle since Gore v. Bush. She didn't need nor want anything else.

But Marie Patronite did not like the idea of being rushed, not even by a client of Harley Daull's stature. In her world, the accuracy of the information she peddled was paramount. Long ago, she realized her reputation and her value to future clients always rested upon her last assignment. She moved slowly, cautiously. Her inability to trust others served her well. She double- and triple-checked everything.

Marie learned that Chastain's grandfather, Andrzej Chastanski, was seven years old in 1905 when his family left their butcher shop in Katowice, Poland for America. Like every immigrant family that made its way to America's shores, they sought a place where their fellow countrymen had already put down roots. For the Chastanski family, that was the south side of Cleveland, Ohio, whose mills needed not only Minnesota's iron ore to make steel, but also inexpensive labor. The hard-working immigrants filled the bill. It was in areas like these where the newcomers "gradually" became Americans. They continued to live, work, and worship among their own kind while slowly learning their new language. Other families from Italy, Hungary, Ireland, and Germany joined them. They shared a common purpose and goal: They wanted to be Americans.

The war against the Kaiser furthered the "Americanization" of the new residents as their sons and daughters enlisted in the armed forces to defend their new country. It was ironic that many of these children were sent to die in muddy foxholes in the homelands their families had just left behind. When the "war to end all wars" finally ended, the immigration floodgates opened wider and more Eastern Europeans flocked to the shores of the United States. They were welcomed by their already American relatives. Alexander's grandfather was twenty-one in 1919 when Congress passed the 18th amendment to the Constitution and thus began the "noble experiment" of Prohibition.

That created an opportunity for Andrzej. He knew his fellow Poles, mostly iron workers, would never abstain from their vodkas. They came to meet after hours, and especially on weekends, in the back room of his father's Fleet Avenue butcher shop where they could play their Polish card games and consume their favorite beverage in privacy and safety. The responsibility to procure their liquor somehow fell to Andrzej and the neighbors began to rely upon Andrzej for their home stocks as well. The profits generated from the back end of the store dictated to Andrzej his time was better spent in the sale of liquor rather than kielbasa. Because of his Polish heritage, which in no manner frowned upon the consumption of alcohol, he could not conceive his conduct was in any way criminal. It was helping him secure his future at a much faster pace than his father could ever have foreseen when he brought Andrzej and his siblings to America.

His reputation and standing in the community grew as fast as his illegal distributorship. After the "noble experiment" had failed, Andrzej encountered very few problems crossing over to legitimate distribution. By 1939, he controlled the sale of beer and wine throughout the greater part of Northern Ohio and was becoming a very wealthy man.

Status, unfortunately, did not come with wealth. He desired to move in different "circles" but his Polish Catholicism and heavily ethnic, funny-sounding last name held him back. He began a transformation by re-naming his business: Andrew Chastain Distributing. Andrzej, now Andrew, took on his wife's religion and in 1940, his only child, a son given the Anglo name Alton, was christened in the Protestant church, further distancing him from his Polish Catholic roots.

Alton Chastain, the senator's father, was most fortunate for the son of a Polish immigrant. His life did not include working in a steel mill or a warehouse or driving a beer truck. Alton had two choices, law or medicine, and his father preferred law and public service. Alton grew up having little say in his future. He attended the best private schools. His father bought Alton's way into an Ivy League college and then law school where he graduated near the bottom of his class. His classmates were amazed when he "landed" the plum job as law clerk for the senior justice of the Court of Appeals for the District of Columbia but not so much when he was appointed a federal prosecutor for the Northern District of Ohio. It was, therefore, a small step when he ascended to the federal bench, which he still occupied when young Alexander himself entered law school.

The transformation was complete in three generations: from Andrzej Chastanski, first generation immigrant and illegal bootlegger to Florida Senator Alexander Chastain, son of retired Federal District Court Judge Alton Chastain, and viable presidential candidate.

Iraq

The Green Zone, also called "The Bubble," was a heavily guarded area of closed-off streets in central Baghdad. At its core sat Saddam Hussein's former presidential complex. The Zone was a nearly self-sufficient "mini-city," defended with chain-link fences, razor wire, earthen barricades and armed checkpoints. Most Americans would be surprised to learn that it is a rather lush tropical area with little humidity and world class date-producing palm trees. The United States set up its headquarters within the Zone at the Convention Center, some of its offices being converted into barracks for U.S. troops, including T and Sally's unit. The Iraqi Governing Council was also within the Zone, now headquartered in a handsome marble structure that once was Saddam's Military Industry Ministry run by his son-in-law. The remainder of Baghdad was referred to as the Red Zone and one of its most dangerous districts was Sadr City.

"Shanks, what the hell are you talking about?" asked T.

"The guy asked me about The Peacock Angel, man—the Yazidis."

Stuyvesant Shanks was from Pittsburgh and the most seasoned veteran of the unit, a career man. Every man in the unit, including those who outranked him, looked up to Shanks. He was on his third and last tour and was, by far, the most knowledgeable member of the outfit.

"I still don't know what you're talking about," said T.

"It's some wild shit, man. The Yazidis believe they were created separately and are descended from Adam...just Adam...not Adam and Eve like the rest of us. They keep themselves isolated. Most of them are Kurds from the northwest province. They believe their Supreme God created the world but left it to seven angels and the Peacock Angel is their main dude. They don't eat lettuce and can't wear dark blue clothes. They intermarry…cousins. Saddam hated them like Hitler hated the Jews."

"They don't eat lettuce? What the hell are you talking about?"

"Go online and enter the name Khalil Aswad and you'll see what I'm talking about. K...H...A...L...I...L. There's a video. These are some nasty-ass people."

T did exactly that. He learned that in 2007, Du'a Khalil Aswad was a beautiful seventeen-year-old Yazidi girl who committed the sin of falling in love with a Muslim boy. The grainy cell phone video showed her being dragged into a courtyard by a mob of more than 200 Yazidi men who were mercilessly pulling and tugging at her limbs. They threw her to the ground and started throwing rocks. It was the most gruesome thing T had ever seen. They aimed for her head as she curled into a fetal position. You could see the rocks and hear them hit and watch her eyes roll back in her head… until she was motionless.

"Oh, Jesus Christ," T muttered with his hand over his mouth.

"That's what you're fighting for son. They're fuckin' animals. After they stoned her, they tied her body behind a car and dragged it through the streets up in Bashika. They buried her with the carcass of a dog which, to them, is the ultimate disgrace. And you know what the real kicker is? After they buried her, they dug her up and sent what was left of her body to Mosul for an autopsy. She was a virgin. All she fuckin' did was kiss a Muslim boy."

"Jesus Christ."

"Yeah. And those are some of the people we were sent here to save from Saddam. Think they're ready for democracy? Doesn't make too much sense does it? American soldiers getting their balls blown off for this shit?"

"It's bigger than that, Shanks."

"Yeah I know, weapons of mass destruction…'nother fairy tale. It's bullshit, man."

T recalled Chastain's interview of a week ago.

"Never mind that shit," Shanks continued. "We're going Red first thing in the morning so get your act together and get some rest."

"Aw shit, are you kidding me?"

"Nope. Fun and games tomorrow."

"Going Red" was their slang for another patrol outside the Green Zone, another day of being in wide open spaces, sitting ducks for an unknown, unseen enemy. They were going to Sadr City.

Carrie Burk

When it came time to go to Cleveland to see Chastain, Eileen, Carrie's best friend, owner of the day care, bailed. Carrie knew Bobby Lee would object to her going alone so she didn't tell him. She didn't want Bobby Lee tagging along in light of his opinion of Chastain. She was absolutely fascinated by the man.

When Chastain arrived for the fundraiser at the Cleveland Marriott, he followed his normal routine. He surveyed those gathered there, looking for an attractive female. Within minutes, he caught Carrie Burk staring at him as he moved through the crowd shaking hands. He shot her a smile and she smiled back. This was going to be easy, he thought to himself. He winked to his bodyguard and nodded toward Carrie. The bodyguard needed no further instruction; he went over to her and Chastain could see her blush from thirty feet.

Chastain was finishing up his short speech to the Cleveland Democratic Club which followed the consumption of drinks and heavy hors d'oeuvres. "I am going to throw a question out to the group. If anyone has the answer, just yell it out. We are now engaged in a war in Iraq with no end in sight. There were nineteen 9/11 hijackers. How many of them were Iraqi?"

Someone yelled, "All of them!"

"No. Anyone else care to guess?"

Silence.

"The answer is none. Of the nineteen, fifteen were Saudi, one was Egyptian, one was Lebanese and two were from the United Arab Emirates. Fifteen were Saudi, ladies and gentlemen. Osama bin Laden is Saudi. *The New York Times* reported that just a few weeks after 9/11, Saudi intelligence had conducted a poll of educated Saudi men between the ages of twenty-five and forty-one. Ninety-five percent of the men polled expressed their approval of bin Laden and his agenda. Ninety-five percent! Yet, the Saudi family has done less than nothing to investigate terrorist links within their kingdom. And the present Administration sent us to war in Iraq. This makin' any sense to anyone? I promise, when elected, I will put an end to this nonsense once and for all. America can no longer afford the human and financial toll of a war that should never have been waged and cannot be won!"

The words were met with loud applause.

Thank God that's over, Chastain thought. Now we can have some fun.

Carrie was invited to join the Chastain "insiders" in the private dining room behind the bar. And when the senator approached her, she swooned like a thirteen-year-old. The man totally intoxicated her with his good looks and charm—the next President of the United States!

Carrie had had several drinks, and two hours later, she did not resist when Chastain led her to his sleeping quarters at the back of the campaign bus. Once inside, she closed her mind to everything and everyone not within that room. It was not that she had abandoned Bobby Lee in her heart.

Rather it was that her heart had discovered within itself chambers of greater capacity, and her thoughts occupied those chambers. She wanted Chastain, all of him. She cared about nothing else. She wanted him inside her.

When he began to unbutton her blouse, she deflected his hand. For a second, he was confused but her eyes never left his. She began to unbutton it herself and Chastain smiled. She fondled him and they fell to the bed where she guided him inside. For her, it was incredible, just as she imagined it would be. And once was not enough. Chastain was as good a lover as he was a charmer, a talker, and a fraud. After an hour, he left Carrie in the bed asleep. On his way out of the room, he winked to his bodyguard and nodded back toward the door. The bodyguard smiled as he went in.

Carrie Burk had been ensnared by her own lust. The bus was rolling down the interstate at 65 miles per hour. There was no one to call out to and no way out of that room. At first, she thought Chastain had returned to lay with her for the night and she smiled. Then she realized the horror about to unfold. There was absolutely nothing she could do. The bodyguard was huge and well-muscled. He flipped her over because he didn't want to look into her face and humped her hard like a dog. She bit her lip to keep from screaming. She knew punishment was being meted out for the betrayal of her husband, a husband whose love for her was without bounds. Then she shut down her mind and thought no more.

He did not take long, his semen dripping onto the bedding as he removed himself. The ordeal was finally over.

Then, the third man came in.

Sometime before the fourth man climaxed, she had passed out.

Bobby Lee

When Bobby Lee went to bed just before midnight, he was not concerned. He knew Carrie and Eileen had planned to make a day of it: travel to Cleveland to do some shopping, attend Chastain's rally, get some late dinner at John Q's, and then return to Crawford. Given the travel time, he did not expect them back until one or two, and he promised himself he would not call. He did not want to appear to be checking up on his wife and her best friend. However, when he awoke in an empty bed at four in the morning, he was concerned and he did dial Carrie's cell, only to have the call go to voicemail. *What was going on? They should have been home by now. Did they decide to stay over? No, she would have called to let me know. Car trouble? No, she would have called. What should I do? It's four in the morning.*

As much as he hated to...given the hour...he decided to call Eileen's husband, Al. It seemed to ring forever, and Burk was about to flip his phone shut when Al answered. "Al, this is Bobby. Have you heard from the girls?"

"I'm sorry, who is this?"

"Al, it's Bobby Burk. Have you heard from the girls? They should have been home by now."

"The girls?"

"Yes! Al, it's four in the morning. Carrie is not here and she is not answering her phone. Have they called you?"

"Bobby...here, wait just a second. I'll let you talk with Eileen, she's right here."

He handed the phone to his wife. At hearing this last statement, Burk's heart fluttered.

"Bobby, what's wrong?"

"Eileen?"

"Yes?"

"What time did you get back?"

It was the wee hours of the morning, Eileen had been "dead to the world" for hours, and her mind had not yet "engaged." She failed to remember this was the day she had "cancelled" on Carrie.

"Get back? Get back from where, Bobby?"

Bobby Lee was approaching a meltdown. He raised his voice and that startled Eileen. "From Cleveland, Eileen! Where else did you and Carrie go!?"

"Cleveland?" Now Eileen understood. "Bobby, I never went to Cleveland. Something came up and I had to cancel. I let Carrie know a few days ago."

Bobby Lee felt a fear greater than any he had ever experienced, even in Iraq when the bullets were flying. But that was just the first emotion he experienced.

Bobby and his wife never kept secrets. They had been through a lot together and they always shared their deepest thoughts, fears, needs, especially when Carrie was dealing with her depression. *Why didn't she tell me about Eileen not going? I could have taken her to Cleveland. Did someone else go with her? Did she want to go alone? Was she meeting someone? What the hell is going on? What do I do now?* Bobby Lee Burk's real fear, one he never entertained before and one he did not want to face, was this night might change his relationship with his wife forever.

"Bobby? Bobby? Are you still there?"

"Yes. Yes. Look, I have to go. Sorry for waking you. I need to go."

"Bobby?" No answer. Eileen looked at her husband, "He hung up. Al, you need to call him tomorrow or go over there."

Hours later, it was morning and regaining consciousness, Carrie realized she was alone. She did not recognize the room she was in, nor did she comprehend that she was on a bus. She had incredible pain in her lower back and legs, and her vagina was bleeding. Her head was throbbing. She looked at the bed linen stained with blood, semen and urine but she had no idea where it came from or how it got there. She searched for her skirt and blouse and put them on but gave no thought to her underclothes or purse and left them behind. She slowly opened the door of the room and saw the plush interior of the empty bus, but she still couldn't put it together. She just needed to get to her car and go home to her husband.

The bus was in the parking lot of an old refurbished hotel of Italianate architecture. The dark sky provided her no clue as to the time of day. The rain was cold and as she searched for her car, it wasn't long before she was soaked to the bone. Her hair was hanging limp as were what little clothes she had on. Her blouse was totally drenched so that you could see through it. The fluids were dripping down her legs. She walked unnoticed on empty streets. She was in Cincinnati, Over the Rhine, north of Liberty Street, looking for a car that was parked in Cleveland.

At the rear of an overgrown, junk-filled parking lot next to an ancient boarded-up Texaco station, she did find a car, or at least the rusted shell of one. She crawled inside and curled up in a fetal position, shivering as much from fear as from the cold. When she was found later that day, it was assumed she was one of the local whores who may have gotten herself beaten up. She was incoherent, mumbling non-stop gibberish. She was eventually transported to Cincinnati's University Hospital, where she was diagnosed with pneumonia and an "unspecified" mental illness. She was incapable of aiding the doctors there in any way.

University Hospital, Cincinnati

At Cincinnati's University Hospital emergency department, walk-ins were directed to give their information at the "intake" counter in the lobby within fifteen feet of the main entrance. The counter was a bit taller than waist-high with a glass partition above. The day after Carrie's admission, that's where her purse had been thrown, landing at the base of the counter. It was only after the purse was discovered that hospital personnel determined who their "mystery patient" was. Since Detective Robert Knauer had left very specific instructions regarding the matter when Carrie was brought in by the squad the day before, he was the first and only person the hospital staff contacted.

There was no staff to interview about how it had arrived because no one saw anything. Hospital security promised they would check their surveillance tapes and contact him. Knauer did not contact Bobby Lee. Instead, he called the Crawford County Sheriff's office.

"Hello, this is Robert Knauer with the Cincinnati Detective Bureau. Can I speak with the Sheriff?"

"Just a minute please."

"This is Sheriff Gutbrod."

"Sheriff Bob Knauer from the Cinci PD. You guys just put out a statewide BOLO for a woman."

Gutbrod didn't let him finish, "Carrie Burk!"

"Yes."

"Oh, thank God! Please tell me she's alright."

"Sounds like you know her."

"Her husband owns the local gun shop. He's been going berserk. Please tell me she's okay."

"Well, she's at University Hospital downtown. She was found in one of the worst neighborhoods in the city. Barely had any clothes on. Doc says she's got pneumonia—she'd been outside in the rain all day...hasn't been able to talk with us, and when she was found, there was no identification, no way for us to determine who she was."

"You say you're from Cleveland?"

"No, Cincinnati."

"Cincinnati!?"

"Yes."

"How the hell? She barely had any clothes on?"

"What little she had on was drenched."

"How'd you get an ID?"

"This morning someone threw her purse into the emergency lobby."

"Any idea what happened to her?"

"No, but the rape kit was positive."

Silence.

"Sheriff?"

Silence.

"Sheriff?"

"Oh, Jesus Christ!"

"Sheriff, any idea why she's in Cincinnati?"

"No. Husband says she went to Cleveland. Was supposed to go with a friend but he thinks she ended up going alone. We contacted the folks up there but got nothing."

"Well, how'd she end up down here?"

"No idea. Any marks on her?"

"No marks of a struggle. But some damage to the vagina...either rape or just rough sex."

"Oh, Jesus Christ! Bobby Lee..."

"Sheriff, any issues there?"

"You mean, with her husband?"

"Yeah."

"My Lord, no. He absolutely worships her. Everyone who knows them, knows that."

"You spoke to Cleveland?"

"Yes; absolutely nothing. No evidence she was ever there. How did you get ahold of her purse?"

"Someone threw it in the ED lobby. Need to check the tapes."

"What about her car?"

"Haven't found it yet."

"What's your plan?"

"Not sure right now, other than to talk with the husband. Are you certain he has no issues here?"

"Yes, no issues, Detective. I'll vouch for him. Can I give him your number?"

"Please. But please keep the specifics to yourself and let him know we'll want to talk with him when he gets down here."

"I'll have him call you immediately."

"Thanks, Sheriff. Say, any idea why she went to Cleveland?"

"Political rally of some sort."

Burk's SUV was on the highway within fifteen minutes of his call to Detective Knauer who gave him directions to Cincinnati's University Hospital and made arrangements to meet him there. Knauer informed Burk his wife had been diagnosed with pneumonia because that was the extent of the information he thought prudent to share. The rest of it, the detective knew, could be disclosed only when the two men could talk face to face.

On flat, straight stretches of the interstate, Bobby Lee's vehicle was hitting speeds in the nineties, but his mind was racing even faster.

Detective Robert Knauer

Knauer left instructions with the hospital staff that Carrie's husband was on the way there and they were to call Knauer as soon as he arrived. Also, the husband was not to see his wife until Knauer got there. Knauer did not want any conversations between the two.

Notwithstanding what Sheriff Gutbrod had to say about the husband, the detective was not ruling out anybody or anything at this point. Too many times he had witnessed a heavily bruised, distraught woman get duped by a boyfriend or husband because "everything was going to change," "everything was going to be alright." He despised any man who mistreated a woman and then came crying to the same woman about how sorry he was. These men weren't sorry at all. They just didn't have the balls to face the consequences of their actions so they begged...and lied...to be let off the hook. They were weak, gutless, women-beaters and, more often than not, they did get off the hook because they understood how desperately their wives or girlfriends wanted to believe "things were going to change."

Knauer recalled one such case not too long ago where the asshole got what he deserved. The husband failed to calculate his brother-in-law's response and he ended up being beaten so badly with a metal pipe that he was unrecognizable. Knauer "maneuvered" the case against the brother in-law so he was charged with nothing more than a misdemeanor; all he had to do was pay a small fine. The husband left town even before the divorce and was never heard from again, and his wife was safe. That was, perhaps, the singular case where Knauer knew justice had been served.

All the detective had to go on so far in this case was a woman who appeared roughed-up, who could not communicate with him, who either had engaged in sex or, more likely, had been raped, who was supposed to be in Cleveland but had somehow ended up at the other end of the State in his city's worst neighborhood. He had noted that she was supposed to be attending some sort of political rally and he was eager to get information from Burk about that. He was also eager to find her car, which he hoped would provide him with information about what had happened. He could not know that two days later, Gutbrod would call to report Carrie's car had been found in a surface lot in downtown Cleveland where it had been sitting for days.

By the time Knauer arrived at the hospital, Burk had been waiting the better part of an hour. He looked like shit and was pissed off because the staff would not let him see his wife. Knauer approached him as he stood by the admission window of the waiting room. Knauer could tell he was ex-military. There was no mistaking it...so at least he and Burk had one thing in common.

"You Mr. Burk?"

"Yes. I want to see my wife."

"I'm Detective Bob Knauer with the Cincinnati Police Department."

"I want to see my wife."

"Yes, I understand. It will be just a few minutes."

"I want to see her now."

"Mr. Burk, the doctors will be right out. I have some information I need to talk with you about."

"It can wait."

"Mr. Burk, we believe your wife was raped."

Knauer would later describe Bobby Lee's reaction to those words as like a man who just had a stake driven through his chest and who knew he was about to die. His eyes froze, staring straight ahead, right through the detective...but seeing nothing. His body was motionless but as if about to fall. His eyes started to tear. Right then, Knauer knew Burk had nothing to do with his wife's situation. Gutbrod was right about this man, there was no question about it. "Nurse, this man needs to see his wife."

"Please come with me."

As the nurse led Burk down the hall, he glanced back at Knauer who was looking for a seat in the waiting room.

Bobby Lee found his wife curled in a fetal position with the hospital blanket wrapped tightly around her face. The way the blanket looked reminded him of the black and white habits nuns used to wear, the ones that hid their hair. Carrie had the blanket clenched in her left hand beneath her chin. Bobby Lee could not see it under the covers, but Carrie's other hand covered her pubic area. Her eyes were closed, and her eyelids were swollen. Her face was ashen and her lips bluish purple like a cadaver. She was motionless.

Bobby Lee started to cry. He pulled a chair up close to the bed and leaned over and kissed her forehead and whispered her name but soon realized any attempt to talk with her was useless. She was somewhere else, not there. He sat next to the bed stroking her forehead and cried.

At the end of an hour, Burk walked out of the room and past Knauer, who caught up with him outside the emergency department entrance. Knauer extended a pack of Camels. "Smoke?" Bobby Lee took one, and Knauer lit it for him, then lit one for himself.

"Iraq or Afghanistan?" Knauer exhaled.

Burk looked closer at the detective. "Iraq."

"Me too. How many tours?"

"Two."

"Me too. Unit?"

"The Big Red One."

"No kidding?"

"Nope."

"You feel like talking?"

"I'd rather listen to what you can tell me about all this."

"I can tell you what we know so far...which isn't much. Can show you where we found her. Haven't found the car yet. No clue how she ended up here. Gutbrod said she was supposed to be in Cleveland at some rally or something."

"Yeah."

"Went by herself?"

"Yeah, I didn't know. Carrie was supposed to go with a girlfriend, but her girlfriend cancelled on her."

"You talk to the friend?"

"Yeah, when Carrie didn't show. Called her."

"Why would she go alone without telling you?"

"Probably figured I wouldn't let her go to Cleveland by herself."

"You could have gone with her."

"Yeah, but she knew I didn't want her to go at all. Pretty much told her what I thought of that asshole."

"Asshole?"

"Chastain."

"It was a Chastain rally?"

"Yeah."

"In Cleveland?"

"Yeah, why?"

"They came through here, too. Day before we found your wife. Went on to Memphis, I think. Any reason she would have followed them down here?"

"No. No way. She was just going to Cleveland for part of the day and then coming back home."

"Okay. We're looking for the car. Gutbrod's BOLO gave us all the information."

"BOLO?"

"Stands for 'be on the lookout' for."

"Got it."

"Look, you'll need a place to stay. There's a Residence Inn not far from here. Take a right out of the driveway and go down to the first light and hang another right. It will be on your left-hand side, about half a mile."

"Thanks."

Knauer gave Burk one of his cards and Burk gave him his cell number.

"Any idea how long you'll be here?"

"No. Depends. Want to get her back home as soon as she can travel."

"Sure. Well, I will let you know when we find out anything. If you have any questions, my cell is on the card there."

"Thanks."

Two days later, Forensics reported to Knauer that the video from the hospital was of no use. No matter how they tried to enhance it, it was just too grainy, and it revealed nothing of value to the investigation. Matters were further complicated when Gutbrod called to tell him Carrie's car had never left Cleveland. Like just about every other investigation, this one started down one path only to reach a dead end, forcing the detective in another direction.

His original thinking that Carrie Burk drove to Cincinnati was apparently incorrect. As he re examined the evidence, he concluded he was now investigating a kidnapping as well as a rape. The timing of Carrie's purse being thrown into the emergency department led him to believe the perpetrator was from the area. Could it be that someone from Cincinnati had driven to Cleveland to this rally, saw Carrie, kidnapped her, and brought her back and...at some point in time, did the rape? But why would anyone travel to Cleveland to see this Senator Chastain if he were coming to Cincinnati the next day? Perhaps the individual was in Cleveland for some other reason and just happened to see her, the campaign's itinerary nothing more than a coincidence. And why would the deed-doer give up the purse? Or could it be that the person who "turned it in" was somehow someone who had nothing to do with the crime?

The car thing had him confused, and when the final report on the rape kit revealed multiple DNA, he truly had no idea what he was dealing with. He needed to talk more with Bobby Lee and he also needed to interview Carrie's friend who was supposed to accompany her to Cleveland. What he really needed was for Carrie to come around and be able to communicate with him and tell him where she was and what had happened.

Knauer and Burk spoke several times over the three days Carrie remained at University. When Knauer shared the lab's final DNA findings with him, Knauer could sense his rage. Knauer understood Burk was the type of man who would not let the violation of his wife pass without retribution...like the fellow with the lead pipe who avenged his sister. For that reason, the detective was relieved when Bobby Lee left for home with his wife as soon as she was able to travel. He didn't need an enraged husband taking matters into his own hands or mucking up his investigation, especially a gun shop owner with a military background.

Sadr City

Some of the most intense fighting of the war was being waged in the Thawra District of Baghdad, popularly known as Sadr City. It was a public housing project built by Prime Minister Abdul Karim Qassim but neglected by Saddam Hussein. It was home to some three million Shiites including the popular young rebel cleric Muqtada al-Sadr, after whom it had been renamed. After Saddam's capture and execution, at the time T's unit was deployed, most of Baghdad outside a Green Zone was under the control of Al-Qaeda. Sadr City was under the control of the Mahdi militia. Suicide and car bomb massacres occurred almost daily.

T's unit was ordered into this man-made hell because mortar attacks were being launched on the Green Zone from within Sadr City.

The unit's objective that day was to find and destroy the source. Problem was they had no real idea who their enemy was: Al-Qaeda or Mahdi for sure—if they could be identified. Even better-hidden were the "civilian" sympathizers of these groups including members of the Baghdad police force. How do you fight an unrecognizable enemy who surrounds you the moment you leave your barracks?

Shanks had been through the drill so many times he had become hardened to it. Unlike Sally and T, he no longer experienced the trepidation of the vigil the night before; he slept soundly. His job the next day was to keep his unit focused, on task, and above all, safe. When his troops were gathered and ready to embark, Shanks would inspect them, outline their objective for the day and then give them a "pep talk." He wanted to remind them, regardless of that day's assignment, the unit's primary goal was to have every man return. He had to give his little speech so many times it became routine but, at the same time, it lifted morale. It lifted morale because he always concluded his little talk using a George C. Scott quote from the opening scene of the movie "Patton." After hearing it for the second time and understanding it was Shanks' regular MO, the soldiers eagerly waited for it and all loudly joined in: "Remember, no bastard ever won a war by dying for his country!" And then, off they would go, trying to avoid doing just that. Shanks recognized it became a rallying cry for his men and it lifted their spirits so, at the end of every address, he would simply say, "Remember..." and let the men loudly shout out the rest. It was like Dirty Harry saying, "Go ahead..." and everyone in the entire world knowing what the next three words were.

The unit's first objective was to establish a position outside the wall that protected the northeast quadrant of Sadr City and work from there. Shanks was forced to lead his men on foot along one of the most dangerous corridors within Baghdad, a route that had been the sight of several engagements with the insurgents. The road was so damaged it was barely recognizable as a road. Mortar and IED craters abounded. There was no activity but that did not mean it couldn't start at any second and come from any direction. Like other seasoned leaders, Shanks emitted confidence as he directed his men. He hid his fear.

They slowly walked toward the wall. T was slightly behind and to the right of Sally as they approached a bend to the west, a bend they could not see beyond.

The IED was placed at that point in the road and was powerful enough to blow up a Humvee. When Sally's right foot depressed its pressure plate, he knew what it was and he looked for the last time...at his best friend T...and mouthed his name. The deafening explosion sucked up every bit of air for thirty yards. T felt the scrap metal tear into his left side. The pain was excruciating. A split second later, he was hit square in the face by what, he did not know. He looked to the new crater in the road, where Sally had been, and saw Sally's helmet rolling away...with his head still in it. That was Tony Icovatti's last memory of Iraq.

Ten days later, Tony came out of the coma at the Army Hospital in Wiesbaden. He had a gauze patch over his left eye, and what little he could see out of his right was blurred. A similar bandage covered what remained of his left ear. The first thing he thought to do was reach for his dick, and thank God Almighty, it was still there. He did not feel for his left leg that had been severed above the knee. His mouth was dry and his throat felt like he had swallowed a box of cement nails. Before he drifted back out, he whispered hoarsely to himself, "Aw shit...Sally."

It was a roadside bomb that took T's leg. But it was Sally's gruesome death that would eventually take his mind.

The Triumphant Return of Salvatore Colonna and Anthony Icovatti

The obituary read:

> *Army Private First Class Salvatore C. Colonna was killed in action by a roadside bomb October 18th in Thawra Province, Iraq. Salvatore is survived by his father Sam and mother Angela of Crawford County and siblings Sam Jr. (Maria), Angela (Dante), Joseph, Elena, and Paolo. His paternal grandparents also survive. He was a graduate of St. Boniface High School in Crawford where he lettered in football and baseball. He was a National Merit semifinalist and planned on attending Bowling Green upon his discharge from the military. He was on his first tour of duty in Iraq. Arrangements are being made through The Moretti Funeral Home and will be made public when finalized. A Mass of Christian Burial will be scheduled for St. Rocco's Church with internment at St. Rocco's Cemetery. An article commemorating Salvatore's life appears on the front page of today's Metro Section.*

For two days, in the high school gymnasium, what remained of Sally's body rested in a closed coffin, draped with the American flag, surrounded by the six members of the Army Honor Guard in their dress uniforms with snow white gloves. It took that much space and that much time to allow all the rural folk of Crawford and the surrounding counties to file by and pay their respects.

On the morning of the funeral, billowy white clouds were set against a deep purple-gray sky without a trace of the sun. The temperature had dropped severely following the downpour the night before, and a stiff, cold wind cut against the faces and watery eyes of the high school students. The entire student body lined the driveway from the gymnasium entrance to the road and then down the road toward St. Rocco's Church. As the students watched the casket being lifted into the horse-drawn hearse of black mahogany, there was only one sound—the flag, half-way up its pole, being whipped by the stiff wind.

The other mourners took their stations along the procession route where the high schoolers had left off. Many of them held small American flags. When the hearse, flanked by the Honor Guard, slowly passed, each mourner standing to the side of the road dropped in behind, and the small procession grew with every step until there were over two thousand slowly making their way to St. Rocco's. VFW members, some in uniform, stood at attention on a corner and saluted the horse-drawn hearse as it gradually maneuvered through the turn. Every law enforcement unit in the county was there to help, and they saw to it the veterans standing at attention on the corner entered the procession right behind the hearse and in front of the Boy Scout troop. Two of them sat in wheelchairs with blankets draped across feeble legs, but their comrades had no trouble keeping up, pushing them along in the slow procession. Patrol cars were stationed at the intersections with their red and blue lights flashing but not a siren was heard. It was surreal: the whiteness of the clouds set against the blackness of the morning sky—like a canvas of a tormented Van Gogh. There were thousands in the "dead march" but there was not a sound save for the clip-clop of a singular horse and the buffeting of a wind so cold it made tears sting.

The post-funeral meal had to be relocated to the Elks Lodge to try to accommodate the mourners. Every member of the St. Rocco's Women's Guild was at the Lodge, but when the hearse approached, they halted their preparations and went out to the sidewalk in their aprons, some still holding kitchen towels. Sally's mother had long been one of their members and almost every one of them had fond memories of Sal, most dating back to the day he was born. Two of them were his babysitters and several were his teachers; not one of them could keep from crying. After the hearse passed by, they returned to the task at hand and solemnly completed their preparations in total silence.

The Mass was going to be concelebrated by three priests. Father DiNardo knew the small church could hold only a fraction of the assembly, so he instructed the Knights of Columbus to set up as many chairs as possible on the parish lawn and in the parking lot where those who did not gain entry to the church could hear the ceremony piped to them from temporary speakers. He had hoped for an Indian summer day but did not get it. What he got was an eerie darkness, a sharp wind, and the constant threat of a storm. He took some consolation knowing St. Rocco's Cemetery, where Sally would be laid to his eternal rest, was only five hundred feet from the sanctuary where the priest was now donning a purple chasuble and two altar boys were filling the censer. Father DiNardo watched them in silence and thought to himself it wasn't very long ago that Sal was one of those boys.

Anthony Icovatti was not there.

Sally was probably looking down on the whole affair and, had he been able, would have warned the young boys and girls who were awed by the pageantry of the event; the evenly folded American flag being presented to his mother, the gun salute, the playing of Taps by the lone bugler, and those goddamned white gloves. He would have appeared to them, right in their faces, only as a head with a ragged bloody neck-to scare them from their thoughts. He would bleed on them and he would scream: "Remember, no bastard ever won a war by dying for his country!" And then he would make a hideous laugh and do anything he could do to prevent them from following his path, which had ended at the cemetery of St. Rocco's with clods of dirt being dropped onto a coffin containing only his head.

The Trip to Washington.

Tony's parents, Bettino and Donata Icovatti, could not attend Salvatore's funeral Mass. They had left for Washington's Walter Reed Hospital the day before. Sally's parents wanted to wait for Tony's return to bury their son, but no one in the military could tell the Icovattis when Tony would be coming home. So that's how it came to a quiet end. After spending their lives together, the two young men were finally going their separate ways. Sally was leaving for good and Tony was not there to see him go.

It was a nine-hour drive from Crawford to Washington, but, years later, Donata would say she remembered little of it. She did recall the guilt she felt leaving her good friend, Angela Colonna, who would have to stand in the cold at St. Rocco's to wait for her son's hearse.

Donata also knew that regardless of what was waiting for her and Bettino in Washington, Angela would trade places with her in a heartbeat if only God were to give her the chance.

The military reported Tony was "seriously injured" by the same roadside bomb that had killed Sal, but Donata did not know what that meant. For nine hours she clutched her Rosary but said not one Hail Mary. She thought only of her son, from his days as a toddler to the day he announced he and Sal were "joining up." She recalled the arguments with T and Bettino and how she finally gave in. She cursed herself. When it became too much, she would lean her head back on the seat and close her eyes to try to hold back the tears as Bettino drove on toward Washington. The nine hours in the car was a trip down "memory lane" no mother should have to make.

The flight Tony was on landed in Maryland twenty minutes before ten. The C-141 Starlifters transporting caskets and wounded always arrived at Andrews Air Force Base in Maryland or Delaware's Dover after dark. The flight from Germany could take up to ten hours and there was a six-hour time difference, but why always after dark? The official explanation from Air Mobility Command was that missions departing Germany had to comply with "airfield operational restrictions," whatever the hell that meant. The Command also explained that doctors in Germany needed additional time to stabilize their patients for the flight. The truth was, the first Administration to commit troops to the Iraq hell-hole enforced a ban on photographs of caskets arriving at American airfields. When the news images shifted to the returning wounded, which were even more numerous, their transport times also shifted.

Back in the year 2000, General Henry Shelton, then Chairman of the Joint Chiefs, introduced to his Harvard audience the "Dover test," named after the air base where the majority of the coffins were off-loaded. Shelton proposed America's politicians should not send young men and women into harm's way "unless America was prepared for the sight of our most precious resources coming home in flag-draped coffins." The politicians ignored Shelton and his "Dover test" by ensuring the dead and wounded returned under the cover of darkness. Decades before, Vietnam veterans complained about returning to a thankless nation. It was worse for the casualties of Iraq: When they returned, they were invisible. Tony Icovatti was among them.

At Walter Reed, the Icovattis were directed to wait near an entrance far from and out of sight of the main emergency entrance. They were struck by the fact so few people were waiting with them. They failed to comprehend that many of the returning soldiers came from families too far away or too poor to make the trip. They were impressed by the hospital staff as well as the military personnel whose job it was to assist the families in any way they could. It seemed like their every need and every question had been anticipated. But the staff's efficiency only reinforced Donata's fear about how insignificant Tony was. They had been through this nighttime drill hundreds of times, meeting thousands of returning wounded...and her son was only one of these. What was his future?

The white school buses had "Walter Reed" stenciled in black on the front. There were three of them converted into ambulances to transport the wounded from the airfield to the hospital. Once they stopped in line at the side entrance, the hospital nurses and their assistants, under the direction of one doctor, went about their business in total silence.

Only the first bus opened its doors and the soldiers began to file off. It was somewhat encouraging to Donata because only a few needed the assistance of the staff. It was after the second bus had opened its doors when she realized the wounded had already gone through a triage of sorts. It was evident the passengers from that bus were more severely injured. She watched the other mothers who had come as they tearfully, and carefully, embraced their children and walked with them into the hospital.

As she waited for the third bus to open its doors, she saw one mother look back at her, and she would never forget the look on the woman's face. It was only then Donata realized she and Bettino were the last ones standing outside. It was the rear door of the last bus that had to be opened....to allow for the width of the gurney. She prayed to the Mother of God. She needed Bettino to hold her up as she watched the gurney receive the personal attention of the doctor and more than half the entire staff assembled that evening. She knew who was on that gurney.

The Reunion

On a Saturday, a month after Tony had finally returned to Crawford, the weather wasn't the best, but it appeared to Bettino and Donata that Tony was having a "good" morning, so they suggested they go to St. Rocco's. Funny how they started rating Tony's days. The last time Donata engaged in such an exercise was when she was caring for her eighty-seven-year-old mother after her father had passed. Now, they found themselves doing the same for their twenty-three-year-old, one-legged, one-eared son.

Sometimes, when it was bad, it was like he was catatonic. Sometimes, when it was really bad, he became abusive. On good days, he was less withdrawn and depressed. Sometimes he had conversations with himself. But nights were always dreadful. He rarely escaped the nightmares. The Icovattis did not know what to expect each morning and, more often than not, their entire day was governed by their son's mental disposition.

The sky was dark and heavy. It was as if the clouds were connecting themselves to the earth. By the time Tony was ready to go, a drizzle had started. It became so cold it was almost sleeting. Donata wanted to reconsider, but she saw the look on Tony's face and said nothing.

Tony lifted his head for the first time when Bettino turned off the ignition. Father looked back at the son and nodded toward a small hill to the right...and the fresh grave. At first, Tony could see little through the raindrops on the car window, but when he recognized where Sally had been "laid to his eternal rest," he began to chuckle.

The parents stared. His reaction frightened them.

Tony saw the look on his mother's face. "Mrs. Whitmarsh," Tony said.

"Mrs. Who?" Donata asked.

"Mrs. Whitmarsh...fat old Mrs. Whitmarsh. Sal is right next to her. Sally and I served her funeral Mass. She was so fat the pallbearers had a helluva time with her casket, and they dropped it going up that hill. Sal and I couldn't hold it in. I could see he was biting his tongue to keep from laughing. He actually had tears running down his cheeks. He told me later he peed his underwear. I got in trouble because I was laughing at Sally trying everything he could not to laugh. Father DiNardo was really pissed at us after the service and said he would never let us do another funeral. But he had to because the damn incense always made the other kids sick. Shit...Sal's lying next to fat-ass Mrs. Whitmarsh."

Tony left the car and began his slow, one-legged trudge up the hill in the rain.

Donata and Bettino made no effort to follow. This was a private reunion and they had no place in it. Donata held her handkerchief to her wet eyes as she watched her son. It was like watching a bad actor portray a pirate with a wooden leg and a parrot on his shoulder; he had to plod up the hill sideways and rock his body hard from side-to-side to make any progress.

When he got to the top, Tony looked at the headstone. Seeing Salvatore's name and dates, he began to cry.

"Not exactly the homecoming we envisioned, Sal."

"No shit, T..."

"They stuck your ass in the ground next to Whitmarsh—do you realize that?"

"No they didn't."

"What the hell, Sally, she's right there." T was pointing.

Donata looked to her husband; "He's talking to himself."

"Yeah, she's there but my ass was blown to bits. It's not here, you fool."

"Oh yeah, that would be right...forgot."

"No problem. Guess you left a few parts over in that shithole as well."

"A leg and an ear..."

"That sucks."

"Yeah, well..."

"T, you know, Shanks was right."

"Yeah, I know, Sally."

Then they said it together in perfect unison, *"Remember, no bastard ever won a war by dying for his country!"* And they laughed.

"T, did he make it out?"

"Shanks? Don't know. After I got hit by your friggin' head, I was in la-la land for a couple weeks. Don't know what happened to the rest of them. Sally, can you answer just one question for me?"

"Sure, what is it?"

"Did it hurt?"

"What do you think?"

"Don't know. That's why I asked"

"No, T, it didn't. It was so big and so fast, there was no hurt."

"Sal, I'm sorry I…"

"Forget it, T! Don't even go there."

"But if I hadn't..."

"Forget about it, T. Hey, why don't you do this? Buy the plot on the other side of fat ass over there and when it's your time, we'll be on both sides."

"Sal, you're an asshole. But okay, I'll do it."

"Good, and can you do me one other favor?"

"Sure Sal, what is it?"

"Don't forget about me out here by myself. It's lonely here…and cold. Come see me from time to time, will you?"

At this T started blubbering and quietly said as best he could, *"Sure...Sal…you got it...I'll stop by every week…I'm not going anywhere."*

"Great. Thanks. Come by next week."

"Yeah…see you next week"

T was soaked, but he didn't know it. He started down the hill. About halfway down, his prosthesis got stuck in the grass and he went down hard. His mother grabbed the door handle, but Bettino grabbed her.

"Honey, don't. He wouldn't want that."

She knew that was right. She covered her eyes.

When Tony finally got back to the car, he said, "Fat ass tripped me. She was getting even." He had a smirk on his face, though his eyes were swollen and red.

Number One, Observatory Circle

The Queen Anne style home was built on the grounds of the United States Naval Observatory in Washington DC in 1893. But it wasn't until 1974, when Walter Mondale moved in, that Congress voted to make the home the official residence of the Vice President. It was extensively renovated that year, but subsequent dwellers, including Bush, Quayle, and Gore, added their own touches courtesy of the $100,000 decorating stipend each received.

Daull had inhabited the home for seven years but had done nothing in the way of redecorating, figuring out a way to pocket the stipend he had been allotted. The home was over 4,000 square feet and had a sizable office for the Vice President to conduct his affairs, but Harley Daull rarely used it other than for picture-taking sessions or the all-too-rare media interview. He preferred to use the smaller library with the large fireplace at the rear of the first floor, where he and Mylott could engage in their discussions behind thick oak doors and thicker stone walls.

Daull took his latest edition of USA TODAY and sat on the overstuffed couch in front of a fire which had been reduced to embers. He threw a log on top in hopes it would eventually ignite. He routinely perused the newspaper for articles or references to Chastain or to himself. There was a feature article about Chastain's campaign tour on page one among the twelve references Daull found throughout the paper. The Florida senator was mentioned in pieces on foreign affairs, politics, and the economy. Two editorials also referred to Chastain. There was a picture on page three of a smiling Chastain shaking hands with the chairman of the Democratic Party.

He had been monitoring reports of Chastain's tour after the bus embarked a week ago, and he was dumbfounded. In vastly Democratic, blue-collar Cleveland, Chastain touted his family's Polish-Catholic roots and spoke of his ancestors selling kielbasa in their Fleet Avenue butcher shop on the city's south side. In Cincinnati, he talked about his Midwestern, conservative values and his defense of Second Amendment rights. When the tour reached Memphis, he focused upon his life in the South, being a representative of the State of Florida. Upon arrival in Maryland Saturday evening, he reverted to his anti-war message and then attended Sunday services at Baltimore's most popular Protestant Church. In New York, he included several references to his wife and his mother-in-law...who was Jewish.

This guy is a fuckin' chameleon, Daull thought. But then he recalled the advice his father had given him more than thirty years ago. "It's not what you are that is important; it's what people think you are." Chastain was the master, Daull admitted to himself. And the snowball had become an "avalanche."

Daull sat on the couch ruminating over the last seven years of his not-so-public life. His own presidential aspirations had been on hold, exchanged for the high-profile number two position within the Administration that Daull thought would become his stepping-stone to the highest office in the land. After being largely ignored during the first term and realizing he had been duped, he announced to the President he wanted off the ticket. But the President could not let that happen. It would have been a huge blow to his re-election efforts. Daull was called into a meeting with the President and a select group of Party insiders, including the chairman, where the only topic of discussion was Daull's "succession" to the presidency. Details of a plan already "in place" were shared with Daull and he "bit" once more, dumber than a fish that tossed the lure the first time by. Now that his time had finally arrived, "Dull Daull" was watching the Party leaders who had promised him the nomination, one by one, jump on the Chastain bandwagon.

Daull did find a singular reference to himself buried at the back of the paper—a short article in the society section reporting that last week he had accompanied his wife to a DC fundraiser for an animal shelter. How fitting, he thought. His presidential aspirations were on life support, literally "going to the dogs."

He disgustedly threw the paper into the fireplace...but nothing happened. The log had failed to ignite, the fire was out, and the fireplace was growing cold. *Where in hell was Patronite?*

St. Joseph's

It was clear to Tony's siblings that his mental state, rather than improving, was deteriorating. Tony's good days were losing out to his bad days, and his brothers and sisters were now growing more concerned about their parents, who were in denial. The oldest son suggested the family consider St. Joseph's, which was nearby and had a mental health program headed up by a Dr. Michael Berringer. They were certain Tony would qualify for services that could ease the burden on his parents. But something had to be done quickly. Part of the problem was his parents. They continued to believe all their son needed was to be with family and he would improve with the passage of time. They could not deal with the "stigma" of mental disease. On this issue, they were not living in the present.

Tony religiously kept his graveside promise to Sally. But the morning after his most recent visit, he was found by his parents sitting on the floor downstairs with his legs crossed like a kindergartner, blankly staring at a wall that Donata had covered with family photos including several of Tony and Sally together. No matter what his parents did, they could not divert his attention. He was rocking back and forth, eyes fixed on the wall, quietly mumbling to himself a phrase they could not comprehend. It was as if he were in trance, catatonic, oblivious.

After the better part of four hours, they called their oldest boy who brought Tony to St. Joseph's, where he was seen by Dr. Berringer and immediately admitted. It was only then Donata and her husband stopped pretending that "everything was alright."

St. Joseph's was one of those mysterious and foreboding places children would dread as they passed by in the family car, especially children threatened by their parents with being left there should they misbehave. It occupied twenty manicured acres on the outskirts of town, but you could see only a small section of the building as you passed by. It sat far back from the very tall wall that bordered the road, a wall constructed of large blocks of hewn Marblehead limestone now weathered black and streaked with gray. The place reminded children of a wicked fairy-tale castle, where they were certain horrible things happened to its inhabitants. But another human being was never seen. It was as if the building itself were an evil spirit holding power over those trapped within. Its utter stillness scared them. The center of the building was all that could be seen from the wrought iron gates. Its residents remained deliberately anonymous and invisible.

It was a week before Dr. Berringer wanted Tony to have visitors. The doctor knew to expect anything from the military returning from a war zone, and he needed that much time to observe and test Tony so he could diagnose him and then recommend treatment options to the family. During that first week, Dr. Berringer saw the good days and the bad. At times, Tony was coherent and cooperative, at other times, silent and withdrawn, and yet other times abusive and threatening.

Berringer eventually diagnosed Tony as having post-traumatic stress with a component of extraordinarily severe depression.

It was a Tuesday when Bettino and Donata met with the doctor at St. Joseph's. The week before, with Tony gone and just her daughter and husband at home, Donata felt guilty; she enjoyed the return to her normal routines and the freedom from the daily anxiety of not knowing what to expect from her son. When they pulled up to St. Joseph's wrought-iron gate, they had to announce their arrival, not to a person, but to a gray metal speaker mounted on a pole, like the ones at the old drive-in movies. Without any response, the gates slowly opened, which would have confirmed to every child beyond any doubt the place was ruled by an evil spirit, or perhaps some unseen being operating hand controls behind a curtain like the Wizard of Oz. This manner of entrance sent an unintended message to the Icovattis that the facility was now in total control. When they drove through the gate and started up the long driveway, even Bettino sensed they were being swallowed up by a living stone monster; more like entering the castle of the Wicked Witch of the West rather than the Wizard's Emerald City.

Upon entering the facility, but before they made it to the reception desk, they were greeted by Laura Herwick, an attractive, rather tall nurse who introduced herself as an assistant to Dr. Berringer. It was apparent she had been waiting for them and this small display of personal attention, along with their brief exchange on the way to the doctor's office, buoyed their spirits.

"Happy to meet you both. Dr. Berringer asked to meet with you first, before you see Tony. His office is on the third floor."

"Thank you," they replied in unison.

Laura had them follow her down the main hallway to the first bank of elevators.

"Tony's doing really well and looking forward to seeing you."

Bettino responded, "That's good to hear."

"You should know we are very proud to be helping the veterans who are with us. They have a special status here. And you'll find he can't be in better hands; a large part of Dr. Berringer's practice has been spent treating soldiers returning from war zones. Tony is very comfortable with him."

From the manner in which Nurse Herwick used Tony's name at ease, not strained or contrived, it was clear to Donata she had established a relationship with her son in the course of one week. Given that Nurse Ratchet with her lobotomy tools played the leading role in Donata's nightmares leading up to this visit, she now experienced a sense of relief conversing with Laura Herwick.

Dr. Berringer's office in no manner resembled the medical offices the Icovattis knew. Its wallpaper and thick carpeting were warm, earthen colors and the furniture had soft cushions and a subdued oak trim. Its window welcomed the sunlight but muted it through the amber glass figurines resting on its sill. No black and white diplomas or other sterile certificates hung on the walls; instead, the three watercolors brought to mind the impressionism of Monet. There were no books in sight. A vase of fresh flowers sat on a small coffee table and gave the room an airy, fresh fragrance. The very faint background music Donata recognized as Enya. She would later describe the room as "very soothing" which, of course, is just how the doctor had designed it. In her entire life, Donata knew of no greater contrast; it seemed impossible to her such a welcoming place could exist within the black-gray stone walls of St. Joseph's. Like Nurse Herwick, Dr. Berringer stood at the door waiting for them.

Dr. Michael Berringer's tall, lean frame was dressed business casual, dark blue trousers and a yellow V-neck sweater, no tie or monogrammed white coat. He was bald on top but had closely shorn gray-white hair on the sides and a matching mustache. His features were sharp. Wire rimmed glasses were perched on a long nose. His hands were huge. His voice was baritone.

"Welcome. Welcome. Please come in. Thank you, Laura."

He guided Bettino and Donata to the sofa. "Here, sit over here."

"Laura, could you please stay for a few minutes?"

She nodded in response.

"Would you care for something to drink?"

"No, but thank you," Donata responded for both of them.

"Laura?"

"No thank you, doctor."

"Well, I was certainly looking forward to meeting with you. Thanks for coming in. Tony is a special young man and you've done a fine job with him. You must be very proud."

Donata and Bettino were instantly placed at ease and their spirits rose.

"We know this place can seem a bit overwhelming, but you need to know this is the right place for your son at this time. I don't have to tell you he has been going through a trying time, both physically and emotionally and he is a bit frail right now, but I am sure we can help him through it. May I call you Bettino and Donata?"

They both nodded.

"How many children do you have?"

In unison, "Five."

"How wonderful. Are they all in the area?"

Bettino answered, "My oldest son works the farm with me. Two are away at college and Tony's youngest sister is still in high school."

"St. Boniface?"

"Yes."

"Any grandchildren?"

"One."

"Sounds like you have a beautiful family." From his discussions with Tony and the medical records which had come with him, this was not new information for the doctor; however, his first goal was to establish a rapport with these parents and there was no better way than to discuss and compliment them on their family.

"We have been blessed," responded Donata.

"No others in the service, then."

"No, just T."

"Bettino, were you ever in the service?"

"No. Vietnam was just coming to an end. I had a draft number, but I was never called."

"I understand Tony and the Colonna boy did everything together, including joining up."

At this statement, Donata diverted her eyes downward. She brought a trembling right hand up to her forehead.

"You did the right thing by letting him decide, Donata."

Donata realized her body language was easily interpreted and she offered no response to the doctor's statement. That was "her issue," not Tony's, and she wasn't about to have that discussion. Doctor Berringer knew in order to help Tony, this concern would have to be addressed at some time, but he also knew now was not the time. Donata's confidence in him could not be assumed; it had to be earned. He was confident in his ability to gain her trust, but how long that would take, he could only guess. On that score, everyone was different.

"Laura probably told you we have treated many military personnel here at St. Joseph's."

"Yes."

"Well Tony has been with us a little over a week and he and I have met every day, sometimes more than once. We have had some really good discussions. Also, there's been testing to help us gain some insight into what is going on. I think it is pretty clear Tony is reacting to Salvatore's death, the manner in which he died, and Tony's feelings of responsibility for him being in Iraq. I understand Tony has been going to the gravesite frequently."

"Yes."

"Bettino, you brought up Vietnam. Vietnam gave us the first real opportunity to fully explore a constellation of symptoms which is now labeled post-traumatic stress disorder—PTSD. It was a brutal war and soldiers witnessed many atrocities. They saw horrible things happen to their friends as well as their enemies. Because of the way human beings were maimed and killed, many returning veterans exhibited a greatly increased sensitivity to their environment upon their return home. We could not understand their overreactions to certain events until we understood what had occurred in Vietnam. They would react to a loud noise by cowering under a table because the noise reminded them of incoming mortar rounds...that type of thing. Even after being home months, or even years, their only focus was survival; it was as if they never left the war zone and that led to erratic behavior we could not understand....at first."

"We've read about that."

"Tony has it. Tony's is just a bit more complex though. Depression is a part of PTSD and Tony has severe depression. And...he is experiencing deeply rooted feelings of guilt. What we have to do is sort it all out and then come up with a treatment plan."

Donata said, "Doctor, some days he is fine—the old Tony, like nothing is wrong, and then some days it's like he's in a trance. Other times he becomes abusive and next to impossible to be around. It is scary. We never know what to expect."

"Yes, I understand. We have seen the same thing."

"Are you talking medications?" asked Bettino.

"Well, depression is often addressed with antidepressant medication, but the real problem here is that trauma is not simple; we have found it to be much more complex than originally believed. The individual responses to trauma vary significantly, so we have learned it is not a one-size-fits-all type of fix. The goal is to develop a treatment plan which is "customized," if you will, to the individual's specific needs. So accurate assessment of the individual is the key, and that is what we have started here with Tony."

"What kinds of assessments are there?" asked Donata, Nurse Ratchet still occupying her thoughts.

"Good question. There are multiple tools in existence. The Minnesota Multiphasic Personality Inventory has a PTSD subscale. There is also the Impact of Event Scale, the Clinician-Administered PTSD Scale, and something called the Trauma Symptom Inventory. Fancy names. Basically, they are all measures of sorts. The problem is, they all rely upon the individual's accurate self-report of experiences and symptoms. So they are subject to the vagaries of memory or sometimes deliberate manipulation of the information. Believe it or not, one of the best assessments remains the Rorschach."

"What is that?" asked Bettino.

"Ink blot," answered Donata.

"That's right, Donata, the ink blot test. It allows the clinician to gain insight into the inner experiences of the patient without forcing the patient to talk directly about them. The test is more a means to assess his present perceptions. In other words, it's very important for us to understand how the patient is currently viewing himself, his experiences, others around him and the world in general. It helps us understand why the patient reacts to trauma like he does and how he does or does not cope with stress."

"How'd he do on it?" asked Bettino.

"Takes it tomorrow."

"So after that you will come up with a plan?"

"That's right. It may take a bit, but we will study the results and create a treatment regimen. But I need you to understand, we might not get it 100% right the first time out. Most likely we'll have some trial and error and certainly some 'tweaking' is possible. We just have to see how things go. His depression and feelings of guilt must be taken into account. And there may be some meds involved."

"So next week we will have a better idea of what needs to be done?" asked Bettino.

"Yes, we will have to talk some more then. It has to be a collaborative effort and it may take a while, but I'm sure we will be able to help your son. Now, do you have any questions for me?"

Bettino blankly stared at his wife and neither said anything.

Their reaction in no way surprised the doctor; he was certain they were a bit overwhelmed. They had to go home and "absorb" everything that was just discussed. The doctor reached out with a business card and gave it to Bettino. "If you have any questions, here is my card. Just give me a call. I wrote my cell on the back. If I don't answer, I promise I will get back to you within a day. Laura, are you going to take them to see Tony now?"

"Yes."

"Second floor?"

"Yes."

"Okay then." He rose. "Thank you so much for coming in. Please understand that together we will be able to work through this and get Tony well. It is just going to take some time."

They thanked the doctor and followed Nurse Herwick out of the office with renewed spirit.

Three minutes later, Laura gently tapped on the door to room 234 but then stepped aside making it clear to the Icovattis she was not going to be a part of their visit.

Tony's room was best described as a small suite like one of those Residence Inn extended stay places. Like Dr. Berringer's office, it was warmly appointed with earthen colors; thick beige carpeting, pumpkin-colored walls and an off-white stucco ceiling. In addition to the queen-sized bed with its comforter, there was a sitting area with a light brown leather recliner and matching loveseat, an oak coffee table and small desk with a reading lamp on its top, and a wall-mounted flat screen television. The lighting of the room was soft and indirect and the two paintings on the wall were watercolors from a local artist. The window treatment was autumn colors.

Tony didn't say anything but opened the door and embraced his mother when she entered, and Bettino embraced them both. They stood together for a long time.

Donata wiped her eyes before the tears had the chance to reach her cheeks. "Honey, how have you been?"

"Okay, Ma. They treat me pretty well here."

"Well, we just met with the doctor for a little bit."

"Yeah? Whaddaya think?"

"Seems nice enough. How are you getting on with him?"

"Great. Talk with him every day. It's getting better. Still good days and bad days. But gettin' better overall though...I think."

"Digs are pretty nice. How's the food?" joked Bettino.

Donata shot darts at him.

"Food's fine, Pa, except the pasta sucks. How is everybody?"

"Everyone is fine," answered Donata.

They talked for almost an hour—a therapeutic session, not for Tony, but for his parents.

Upon leaving, in the hallway they passed Bobby Lee Burk who was on his way to Room 235.

The *Playboy* Interview

"Senator, let's start by discussing a statement you made about our nation's news reporting agencies. You said, and I'm quoting here, 'What they decide to report and how they go about it affects how Americans perceive their country.' Not sure I understand. Can you give us an example?"

"Certainly. Do you recall the recent news coverage about a helicopter crash near Baltimore? Two people lost their lives."

"Yes. It was carried on the front page of *The New York Times*."

"Do you recall an article in that same paper about how a ferry in Bangladesh capsized and 212 people drowned?"

"No."

"It's not surprising you wouldn't remember it. It was reported in a four-sentence paragraph buried at the bottom of page 8. What does that tell you about our view of the world? Could it be the helicopter story sells papers better than the Bangladesh tragedy? Here's a better example. What do you know about Pan Am Flight 103?"

"Lockerbie. Terrorists."

"That's correct, it exploded over Lockerbie, Scotland, and 270 innocent people lost their lives to a terrorist's bomb including thirty-five students from Syracuse University and eleven people on the ground. How much media attention did that event command and for how many years? But what do Americans remember, or even know, about Iran Air Flight 655?"

"Not sure."

"That was the plane shot down by the USS Vincennes while the ship was operating in the Persian Gulf; they were unable to identify it as a commercial airliner. Two hundred and ninety innocent people, almost all from the Middle East, including sixty-six children, perished. How is it Americans were outraged over the downing of Flight 103 but somehow ambivalent over the human catastrophe our own Navy caused?"

"I see."

"Let's fast forward. Two more examples. The report of a gone-wrong U.S. drone attack which annihilated a Pakistani family was hardly a blip on our national news. Another similar event, where an entire Yemeni wedding party was mistakenly obliterated from the face of the earth by another drone, was little more than a footnote. Think it through! American soldiers are flying remote-control drones armed with missiles over supposedly sovereign nations...and killing innocent civilians. America yawns. Why? Because those were not big news stories in the States; they were just barely mentioned. Most Pakistanis and Yemenis despise our country, and Americans fail to understand why. Ask yourself how you would feel if you were a New Jersey mother of three who just sent your children off to school four blocks away...and you see a Chinese drone laden with bombs being flown in the same direction? The media needs to wake up to what our military is doing 'in the name of democracy' or under the ruse of 'protecting our freedom.' Americans need to understand the utter havoc and upheaval the United States has caused in the region has nothing to do with protecting our freedom. The American men and women who died in the Middle East were not protecting us in any regard; they were the aggressors in someone else's land. Let's look at it for what it really is and stop hiding behind the American flag. And yes, the media bears some responsibility here."

"Those are pretty damning words, senator."

"Yes, they are. But I challenge anyone to prove any country in the region is more stable and that human rights are now safeguarded there because of our involvement. The United States has trampled the rights of other countries and continues to do so to further its illusory and unattainable goal of 'spreading democracy.' When is our country going to figure it out? The answer is: only when it adopts a foreign diplomacy based upon respect for the rights of sovereign nations and a pledge not to meddle in their business. I am the only candidate to offer such an alternative to the electorate."

Tony stopped reading the article right there. That son of a bitch. We were the aggressors? This asshole has to be stopped. He tore the pages from the magazine, rolled them up, and stuck them in the pocket of his flak jacket hanging in the closet.

St. Joseph's

Carrie's condition did not improve. She had been back home, a resident of St. Joseph's, for three weeks. She was still incapable of communication. Eyes were open, but blank...dead...nothing behind them. Like her fellow floor mate, Tony Icovatti, she had been diagnosed with posttraumatic stress disorder, however much more severe. It affected her ability to walk, talk, and take care of herself. She was now being fed intravenously. Her husband was there every morning and returned to her bedside as soon as he closed up his gun shop, staying there until sleep came to rescue her. He was at her side all day Sunday, every Sunday. That was his life. He remained totally devoted, but now his fidelity was to a woman who was suffering. But why? What was the true cause? A brutal rape? Or the shame, guilt and regret of having betrayed her husband...a betrayal only she knew? Dr. Berringer had never seen such a critical case and he was deeply concerned. Like Detective Knauer, he desperately needed to get through to her. If he could not identify the demons at work within her, he had little chance of doing her any good. Unless some progress could be made, and soon, her organs were now at risk, her body being the victim of her mind's sickness. He remained in constant communication with Bobby Lee.

In the evening, Bobby Lee would lift his wife into a chair and wheel her out to the television room and that is where Tony first saw the two of them. Like Knauer, he could tell Bobby Lee was ex-military and he wondered what had happened to bring his wife to this place. Watching the couple from the other side of the room, he saw how tenderly Bobby Lee doted upon his wife. Tony wondered about himself and the way he looked now, whether he could ever have such a relationship; to be so in love you gave up your life for someone who acknowledged nothing, responded to nothing, who could not return love to you. He watched as Bobby Lee positioned her next to the couch where he would sit, then arrange her clothing, wipe her mouth and sometimes her nose and talk with her without ever hearing a reply, ask her questions which were never answered, reminding Tony of his little sister having a tea party with her favorite doll. Tony sometimes wondered who was more delusional, Carrie or her husband, but all the while envying Bobby Lee for his love. Tony always made a point to be in the room in the evening to watch them from a distance as everyone else watched the television set. He thought to himself he might be able to help her.

A week later, right after lunch, Tony went to Carrie's room and found her sitting in a wheelchair. Her seemingly blank gaze followed him as he entered the room. When he walked behind her, she turned her head just a bit. He wheeled her to the door, checked up and down the hallway to be sure "the coast was clear," and without a second thought, took her down the hall to the empty television room. He turned on the set but left the volume on low; he wanted the opportunity to speak with Carrie without any interruptions and, if anyone butted in, he could say they were just watching TV. He started their own private little "tea party."

"Hi, Carrie. My name is Tony. I'm in the room next to yours."

She appeared to be looking at his mouth but did not reply.

"I thought since we're neighbors, we should get to know each other."

Nothing.

"Maybe if we talked, we could help each other out."

No response.

"Anything you want to see on the set?"

Blank stare.

He fetched two bottles of water from the small refrigerator in the corner. Perhaps sharing a drink would help her to open up. He twisted off the cap and placed her water in the chair's cup holder.

"Dr. Berringer taking good care of you?"

With this question, an utter look of terror transformed Carrie's face...and it startled Tony. Her eyes were as wide as they could be as she jerked her head into her chest. She quickly lifted both arms to shield herself from Tony's look...so that he could no longer see her expression of horror and repulsion. Her reaction set off his own demons, it reminded him of too many faces he had seen in Iraq, frozen faces attached to human carcasses. And one in particular...which was detached.

Oh my God, why such a reaction?

He quickly turned, half expecting to see someone looking over his shoulder, but there was no one else in the room.

"What is it? Carrie, what is it? Did something scare you?"

She did not answer but cowered lower in her chair.

Tony had no clue. His first thought was she was responding to his mention of Dr. Berringer, but he just as quickly dismissed it; that couldn't be it. He wondered whether his appearance somehow triggered her response, but he dismissed that too: it probably would have happened sooner. His next thought was how naïve he was, thinking he could help Carrie when the professionals at St. Joseph could not. Perhaps taking her out on his own wasn't such a good idea; he had better get her back to her room and right away before anyone saw them. He did not realize what had just happened; he failed to notice whose image Carrie saw on the wide-screen television mounted on the wall behind him.

By the time he got her back to her room, she was curled up in a fetal position, as much as the chair would allow, and there were tears running down her cheeks. He left her there, sitting just like that, and retreated to his quarters as fast as a one-legged man could go, all the while cursing himself for seemingly making matters worse.

Later that evening, he was in his usual spot in the television room, watching Carrie and her husband from a distance. Carrie was unchanged, staring blankly ahead, not responding to her husband's voice or touch. It was six thirty and the national news broadcast was on the set. The reporting of that day's events began with an interview of Alexander Chastain. Carrie jolted upright in her chair, threw her arms in front of her face and then cowered down as low as she could, startling Bobby Lee. Since her trip to Cleveland, this was the only display of emotion he had seen from his wife and obviously a very bad one. And it was the same picture Tony had witnessed earlier in the day. Bobby Lee tenderly put his arms around his sick wife and looked around the room for help. Like Tony that afternoon, he did not see what was on the set. But this time Tony did.

Bobby Lee called for a nurse who saw a writhing Carrie trying to get away from someone or something no one could identify. Except Tony. They got her back to her room where Bobby Lee lifted her from the chair into her bed. And he sat there stroking her forehead into the wee hours of the morning—until she stopped shaking.

The following day, Carrie never left her bed. Things were getting far worse—her mind was not being cured and her body was deteriorating. Before lunch, Tony entered her room once again. This time, he brought with him a two-day-old local newspaper with Senator Alexander Chastain's picture on the front page. Tony entered Carrie's room to see her lying motionless in her bed, staring straight ahead. He then stuck his head back out into the hallway before quietly, slowly closing the door. He moved to the side of her bed and gradually reached behind his back. He unfolded the paper and showed it to Carrie. She immediately curled up like a baby and Tony could see both hands reach down to cover her genitals. She rocked violently back and forth and she began to cry. Tony placed his hand on her shoulder.

He said, "Carrie, it's alright. It's alright. It's just a picture. It's alright. Did he hurt you? Did this man hurt you, Carrie?" Tony was unaware of the circumstances which brought Carrie to St. Joseph's, and it was inconceivable to him there could be some connection between the two people. Chastain was a senator from Florida with a strong chance of becoming the next President and she was just a small-town girl from rural bumfuck Crawford, Ohio. Certainly she did not know Chastain, but there was no question she feared him.

There was no answer from Carrie. She pulled the covers tightly around her face and buried her head in the pillow.

Tony found a pen on the nursing chart hanging on the wall, scribbled on the front of the paper, left it on the stand next to Carrie's bed, and returned to his room.

When Bobby Lee arrived for his visit four hours later, his wife was still curled up in a fetal position. It was some time before he noticed the folded newspaper on the nightstand; he so concentrated on his Carrie. When he did open the paper and saw what Tony had written on it, he was puzzled. *Where did this come from? Whose writing is this? What did this person know?* With some hesitation, however, he followed the directive. He slowly placed the paper in front of Carrie's seemingly blank eyes.

She straightened right out from head to toe like a death row inmate in the electric chair. She screamed. Bobby Lee threw the paper to the floor and collapsed upon his wife. He tried to hold her whole body all at once. Bobby Lee now understood. Tony was standing in his room near the door and he heard the scream.

Tony Icovatti

It was over three weeks since Tony had last slept at night, and during the day, he was growing increasingly more agitated. He dressed in his fatigues and left St. Joseph's at two in the morning; simply packed up the small camo duffel he had arrived with and walked out the door, down the long winding drive and through the open man-gate next to the main entrance. The guilt he suffered over Sally's gruesome death was overwhelming him. Their plan was to return home as heroes, not the way they did: Only Sally's head made its way back and in a large coffin—which fooled everyone. And Tony limped back with only one leg and one ear, looking so hideous those who saw him couldn't help but stare. It was Tony's fault, but it was Chastain who kept hammering into Tony's head their extreme losses were "all in vain." Those words reverberated throughout his mind, night and day, every night and day, never stopping, pounding, pounding...slowly driving him insane.

First stop was the cemetery behind St. Rocco's where he left his bag at the bottom of the small hill and trudged up to see Sally. He knelt down on his knee as best he could and started pulling crabgrass from around the edge of Salvatore's headstone. His eyes began to tear as he saw the name in what little moonlight there was.

"Hey, Sal."

"T, how the hell you been?"

"Not too good."

"What's the problem?"

"Dunno. Just not feelin' good right now."

"What brings you here at this hour of the morning?"

"I dunno, wanted to see you before I leave."

"Leave? Where you going?"

"Chicago."

"Yeah? What's the deal?"

"Need a change of scenery."

"Yeah? What's up with that?"

"Dunno. Nothin' much goin' on here I guess."

"Yeah. Never was. When you comin' back?"

"Don't know. Just going to play it by ear."

"That shouldn't take you too long!"

Tony busted up when he realized what he had just said. He laughed so hard, tears started running down his cheeks. When he stopped laughing, he said, *"Go screw yourself, Sally."*

"Wish I could. Don't have the equipment."

"Miss you, man."

"Miss you too. When you get back, make sure you stop by."

"Yeah, for sure."

"Take care of yourself."

"Yeah. Will do. See you when I get back"

"Yeah, I'll still be here."

At this, T was blubbering-more tears, but for a different reason.

He started walking, not toward home but north toward the entrance to the turnpike, where he stuck out his thumb and got picked up by a young man in his truck on the way to Gary. The road would eventually get Tony to Chicago, the sight of the next Chastain rally. He wasn't even sure why he was going or what the hell he was going to do once he arrived. He had a little over three hundred dollars on him which certainly wouldn't last long but...he didn't care. He wanted to eyeball Chastain close up and maybe say a thing or two to him. He didn't know; perhaps it would make him feel better, but he really didn't know. All he knew was he had to go.

The last leg of his trip, from Gary, Indiana into Chicago, was via Greyhound. The bus had started out from Erie seven hours before and was almost full. When he took the empty seat near the front, T failed to notice the four young men at the very back of the bus who were wearing camo fatigues. But they noticed him.

A deep sleep finally came to Tony and when the bus pulled into the terminal, he felt he had been in a time warp; he had closed his eyes in Gary and only moments later opened them in Chicago. As the other passengers disembarked, Tony took his time to wake and get his bearings. The last passengers to exit the bus, the four young men from the back, acknowledged Tony as they walked past his seat toward the front exit.

The four were busy retrieving their bags from the bus's baggage compartment when Tony finally trundled down the front steps of the bus, clutching his duffel. The tallest of the four, the one with only one arm, got the attention of his three friends and nodded toward Tony. They watched in silence. After they got their stuff, they caught up to Tony just inside the terminal.

The tall one asked, "Iraq or Afghanistan?"

Looking at the man's empty sleeve which was pinned to the sidc of his camouflage jacket, Tony responded, "Iraq, Sadr City. You?"

"Fallujah. IED?"

"Yeah."

"Me too. Where you headed?"

"Don't really know just yet."

"You here for the rally?"

"Yeah...Chastain."

"Us too. Got a place to stay?"

"No."

"Look, we hooked up with a couple guys who have a place on the south side and we're going to crash with them. I'm sure you'd be welcome to come along. Might have to sleep on the floor but it saves the bucks."

"Wow. Sounds great."

The tall one extended the only hand he had left, "Name's Tim Neary."

Taking his hand, "Tony Icovatti."

"This here's Mike Tharp...and Tommy Weybrecht...and John Paciorek."

All three of them shook hands with T.

They made their way to the parking lot where a rather old, beat-up Dodge Caravan had been waiting for them, driven by another Middle East veteran named Scott. Neary explained to Scott they had just met Tony on the bus, and he was in Chicago for the same reason they were. He was immediately welcomed. On the way to Scott's apartment, Tony learned this small group had been traveling the country for almost a year, staging protests in cities wherever Chastain was scheduled to speak. They told Tony they were part of a much larger network of veterans, some even Vietnam era, who supported them with meals and places to stay and sometimes accompanied them for part of their trip. They joked about how much beer and pizza they had consumed over the last twelve months. Right then, Tony had no idea he would become a member of this group and travel with them for the next three months, shadowing Chastain wherever he went. He also had no idea Neary and his small band had been on the radar of the NSA for months and were on the FBI's "watch but don't encounter" list. His ignorance would later cost him dearly.

Number One, Observatory Circle

Harley Daull and Chester Mylott were back in the small library on the first floor of the Vice Presidential residence where they conducted most of their business rather than use Daull's spacious, but less private, office. They preferred to operate behind the stone walls and thick oaken door which separated the library from the office and the remainder of the first floor. They were watching the end of the latest Chastain speech on the television set.

Marie Patronite had been summoned by Mylott to report on her "research." As Mylott and Daull were conferring in the library, she was sitting in Daull's office outside its doors. Being in the residence brought back a flood of memories; she had been in the vice-presidential quarters many times in her youth. Her mother had become close friends with the Vice President's wife—the two women had much in common—and she had brought a young Marie there often. Sometimes they would accompany Marie's father, the senior senator from Connecticut. Marie would play hide-and-seek with the Vice President's children as the wives visited and the husbands conducted business. Marie had been all over the house and she knew of every nook and cranny, including the original wood plank liquor cabinet in the corner of the office. When the home was built in 1893, the cupboard was cleverly designed to be accessible from both the office and the library. The novelty of it and its dark, rough-hewn beauty saved it from every remodeling venture over the years. Marie knew you could open its door in the office and peek through its back wall into the library. She walked over to the cabinet and opened its door just a bit, hearing Chastain's speech just as clearly as if she were in the library sitting next to Mylott and Daull. She immediately realized her appointment with Mylott would be delayed until after the speech concluded and that did not make her happy; she was unaccustomed to waiting.

"Ask yourself this; why is it the greatest country in the history of the world has not figured out how to educate its children, provide healthcare to all of its citizens, and take care of its elderly? Ask yourself why there is not enough money to fund adequate job training and retraining programs for our poor and working poor. Why can't we guarantee affordable higher education for our youth? Why have we fallen behind so many other countries in academics? It's not because our country lacks the resources; it is because our country's priorities are cockeyed, completely out of kilter. We prefer to spend billions of our dollars maintaining military bases in foreign lands, fighting unwinnable wars and participating in civil wars we have no business being a part of. Ask yourself how we have come to this point. Why has the United States appointed itself the "policeman of the world"?

"We have fallen behind other countries because their economies, unlike ours, are not strangled by the human and financial toll of making war. Unlike us, other countries do not hold onto the fallacy they must impose their form of government on the entire world. Ladies and gentlemen, democracy may work for us—and some may argue just barely—but our goal of making every other country in the world a democracy is a pointless venture doomed to failure. Until we significantly reduce our foreign military spending and stop meddling in the affairs of other nations to further this imaginary goal, we are doomed to repeat history. Iraq and Afghanistan are Vietnam all over again. Ladies and gentlemen, it is true: Those who do not study history are condemned to repeat it! That is the America we now live in.

"I ask you to consider the answer to this question: How do we get out of this mess we have created for ourselves? The answer, ladies and gentlemen, is new leadership. A new direction. Keep American assets, both human and financial, on American soil. Redirect the dollars we now spend on war-mongering to fund necessary programs and benefits for Americans and to rebuild our nation's crumbling infrastructure. I ask you to dare to imagine what our country would be like should we accomplish such a goal. Imagine what your children's futures would be. Consider the resources that would be at their disposal if only we redirect our focus and goals away from military priorities. We have tried the military way for the last century. Do we now recognize that it does not work? If not now, when? Korea, Vietnam, Iraq and Afghanistan...how many more are there going to be?

"I do not want our children and grandchildren saddled with these problems. And make no mistake about it; if we fail to act, we are going to weigh them down with these same burdens. We have to act now! We have to entertain a whole new way of thinking.

"Democrats have a choice in this primary election. Our party can choose an entrenched, professional politician who clings to the old way of doing things or it can choose someone who dares to dream of a better America for all of its children. I say, let us dream!

"And let me be clear about this. Understand I am not advocating that we jeopardize our national security by gutting our military; our forces must remain strong in order to protect our shores. The last bill I sponsored in the Senate proposed a re-direction of our military spending which will effectively strengthen our country's defenses, not gut them. However, my proposal also recognizes the true cost of protecting our country is not remotely close to what we currently spend in order to bully other sovereign nations and interfere in their politics.

"Ladies and gentlemen, I ask you to join with me and dare to dream, if not for yourselves, for your children. I stand before you and tell you we already possess the resources necessary to make those dreams come true; we simply need to redirect them.

Thank you."

Mylott clicked the remote and Chastain's image faded from the screen. He turned to Daull, "How in hell can anyone argue with that?"

On the other side of the cabinet wall, Marie perked up.

"Can't," responded Daull.

"Well then, how do we respond?" asked Mylott.

The Democratic presidential primary started out as a nine-man race but it was now reduced to four...but really only two. The loud-mouthed, do-nothing congressman from Ohio who never sponsored one piece of meaningful legislation, and the governor from Nebraska with the funny-sounding name were reduced to political footnotes. It was going to be Chastain v. Daull for the nomination but Chastain already had a two-digit lead in the polls. The "Chastain avalanche" was at the top of the mountain ready to be unleashed and Daull was squarely in its path.

"We adopt it as our own. You talk to the Chairman?"

"Won't return my calls. What do you mean we adopt it as our own?"

"You meet with the other guy?"

"Yesterday."

"What's his name?"

"Rhuloc Futrell."

Marie was "all ears." She jotted down the name on the inside of her folder, spelling it phonetically.

"Where's he from?"

"DC."

"Really? What's his deal?"

"Army. Two tours in Iraq and one in Afghanistan. Certified sniper. The guy appears to be incredibly bright but he probably shoulda' stayed in the service. Had some troubles when he got home."

"Good soldiers make lousy civilians."

"There you go."

"So you think he's the right guy for this?"

"Yeah. Like I said, he's a smart guy and an Army-trained killer."

Marie wrote 'DC' and 'Army' on the inside of her folder. She now had a new research project of her own.

"Call him."

"You sure?" asked Mylott.

"Yeah. We have to stop dickin' around. There's only one way to stop Chastain. Then we take up his message."

Marie could not believe what she was hearing. She started to tremble.

"What's he going to cost us?" Daull asked.

"Fifty up front and fifty when it's done."

Marie wrote down "100K."

"Jesus Christ! Well, what are we doin' with what's-her-name?"

"I'm sorry?"

"The broad we're paying to get the shit on Chastain."

"Her name is Patronite."

"Yeah. Whatever. What do we owe her?"

"We've paid her twenty-five and we owe her another twenty-five."

Daull thought for a second. "Tell her we don't need her."

"You're serious?"

Now she was really concentrating.

"Yeah. We can use the money for Futrell."

"You want me to stiff her on the fee?"

"Yeah, we haven't got crap from her, have we?"

"She's supposed to be here today."

"Good. Tell her we don't need her. Tell her we're takin' the high road and we don't need the dirt."

At this, Marie slowly closed the cabinet door and quietly stepped out of the office. She waited for Mylott on the Victorian loveseat in the hallway, the one under the picture of Dan Quayle, another politician who had been "a heartbeat away from the presidency" who could not spell the word 'potato.' Those bastards, she thought to herself. Those fuckin' bastards.

When Mylott finally came out of the office to speak with her, she played it cool. She told him she understood, wished them luck with the campaign, and quietly left the Vice President's residence. She was chomping at the bit to begin her new research project. Tracking down an individual with a military background and an arrest record would be a "piece of cake" and she was anxious to get started.

Rhuloc Futrell

Like so many other veterans, Futrell was unprepared to leave the service. His sole function for years was to kill as many "towel heads" as possible and...he was very good at it. But, like Tony Icovatti, he had witnessed atrocities, the worst being the civilians and especially the children, and the worst part of that was not knowing which side was responsible. Leaving his unit, leaving the Middle East, leaving the military, returning to his small family and his job at a Maryland water treatment plant, all in the space of four weeks, was destined to cause problems.

Within two years, his family's elation over his return had long faded, eventually supplanted by uncertainty and then downright fear. They mistakenly thought their "old" son and husband and father would return to them just as he had left them but that was impossible. He had a whole different reality now which he could not escape. He had, indeed, become a trained killer, just as Mylott had reported to Daull. His family and co-workers failed to comprehend Futrell was still in the war zone, still killing. Troubles with co-workers during the day were followed by arguments at home with the wife. Several times, he had left for weeks on his own, which in due course led to the loss of his job. He now had a tenuous relationship with the family he used to adore and he was on the brink of bankruptcy.

While sitting in a Maryland jail awaiting arraignment on a second spousal abuse charge, Futrell learned of "a dude willing to pay big dollars for a job." Through the efforts of an "intermediary," two weeks later he was meeting with Mylott on the south side of DC, though he did not know who Mylott was or what he did. Two weeks after that, he was in receipt of more money than he had ever seen in his life—fifty thousand cash, with the promise of more and he began to plan the job. He had returned to what he knew best.

Mylott was right about Futrell—he was incredibly bright. He became a student of his new "craft," reading up on others who had gone before him...but not because of a love of history; he simply wanted to avoid the mistakes others had made. He was particularly interested in Lee Harvey Oswald because he was very much like him: a loner, ex-military, and a sharpshooter. What if Oswald had been a bit more intelligent and had planned better? Sneak an untraceable rifle into the Texas Book Depository, squeeze off the rounds without leaving any marks on the weapon, close the window, return the gun to a previously prepared and secure hiding place within the massive building, and quietly rejoin your co-workers as the chaos ensued. Stay employed for several more months before quietly resigning and disappearing "into the woodwork" without suspicion. Oswald had made a lot of mistakes. After he studied Oswald, he began studying his target, Alexander Chastain.

Resource materials available to Futrell were abundant. Over the last six weeks, Chastain had been the subject of the *Playboy* interview, appeared on the cover of *Rolling Stone*, and had almost one entire edition of *People* Magazine devoted to him and his family. Futrell quickly had him pegged: just another silver-spooned, never-worked-a-day-in-his-life, lily-white pretty boy who had everything handed to him. Chastain may have seen pictures of Iraq and Afghanistan in the magazines, but that was as close as he came to those places. Big talker, no balls. But what really infuriated Futrell was Chastain's unrelenting theme: All the American soldiers sent to their deaths since Korea had "died in vain." Who the hell did he think sent these brave men to these Godforsaken places to die? He recognized Chastain as a fake, like other millionaire Democrats, both male and female, who put on white capes and rode white horses and portrayed themselves as "champions of the poor and downtrodden" who, at the end of the day, retreated by private helicopter to their family compounds in places like Hyannis Port, Martha's Vineyard, and Nags Head. Hypocrites all. He grew to hate the man...which was going to make his job a whole lot easier.

He was not overwhelmed by his new undertaking; he simply approached it like the seasoned soldier he was, now charged with another mission, a new objective. Identify the target, study its weaknesses, plan your assault, and maintain your exit route. In the Army, Futrell could execute a "kill shot" from over half a mile away. A high-powered rifle from a distance, much farther away than Oswald stationed himself, was certainly the best alternative. Chastain will be dead before anyone even realizes a shot had been fired. The when and where was really now the issue.

Marie Patronite had no problem securing Futrell's latest arrest record and mug shot. From that, she took his DOB and Social Security Number and retrieved real estate, BMV, banking, and education records. Accessing the military's data on Futrell was simple. Within days, she acquired all the information she needed, which also enabled her to put Rhuloc's face together with his name. The bigger question for her was what to do with it all. Did she not just hear the Vice President of the United States direct his associate to hire an assassin to kill a U.S. senator? What the hell does she do? If she went to the authorities with her information...what does she really have? What law enforcement officer in his right mind would take action against a man of Daull's stature based upon what she had to offer? Her "evidence" would appear to the authorities to be nothing more than an accusation without any real proof and coming from an individual who made a living digging up and selling "dirt" on public figures. No...she really needed much more before she could expose herself to that scrutiny; she needed irrefutable proof, but perhaps she could work at it from the "backside" to convince Futrell to come forward? How dangerous would that be? And while it may have been relatively easy to gather Futrell's personal data, finding him would be an entirely different, more difficult, endeavor and something she never had to do before. She thought about calling her ex, Nick, but she just as quickly discounted that notion. If she did share her information with anyone, even Nick, she would lose total "control" over it and place herself in jeopardy. She had to remain absolutely, one hundred percent confident Daull would never know what she had...until it was too late for Daull. She fully realized for Daull, "desperate times called for desperate measures," and she was certain he would not think twice about removing another "obstacle" in his way. For a split second, her thoughts drifted to her dead father, another vindictive bastard.

She did not waiver: Marie Patronite would get even with the bastards. However, unlike Futrell, it wasn't only the when and where she had to figure out; it was also the how. A man's life could hang in the balance. What she utterly failed to grasp was she was not unlike the father she despised.

The Campaign Trail

Tony was just as active on the campaign trail as Chastain. The small group of veterans he joined in Chicago followed Chastain from Milwaukee to Oklahoma City to Omaha. At every venue, they had the support of like-minded Middle East veterans who had grown tired of the politics. Many of these veterans had "issues" upon their return to the States and scores of them were fighting another war...for benefits and health care. Many of them were dying only because of the VA's criminal futility. Lots of them remained unemployed though they had been back home for months, and some, even for years. Now they were being described as "aggressors in foreign lands." Those who were injured...and the families of those killed in service to their country...were being told by Chastain their efforts were "in vain." Icovatti, who set out to be a hero like Pat Tillman, and who talked his best friend into joining up only to see him annihilated, could not rest. Tony's guilt over Sally's god-awful death was kept in check by his steadfast belief their cause was noble...and he could not let anyone take that from him; it was what kept him sane. The legacy bestowed upon them by this know-nothing politician could not stand; Icovatti had to fight back or risk losing whatever weak grip on reality he still held.

Along the campaign trail, the small group of protestors struggled to redirect the media attention away from Chastain and toward them, if only for a soundbite or two. One-armed Neary, the most outspoken of the men, had been interviewed by local television stations in several cities and, even once, by the national news. He had become "the face" of the returning veterans. The group gained the attention of the NSA and FBI who were assembling a file on each man, including Tony Icovatti. Had the veterans known the extent of the surveillance being conducted, they would have enjoyed the irony. They fought for their country; however, now they were considered something of a threat and their movements were being tracked. But they really hadn't changed at all; they held the same beliefs now as when they joined up.

In Boise, they got into a scuffle with the local police over where they were allowed to station themselves and three of them, including Tony, were arrested for failure to follow a police directive. It was little more than a minor misdemeanor, but now there was an arrest record which included an appalling "mug shot" of a disheveled Tony wearing his flak jacket and revealing heavily bloodshot eyes, scarred and reddened scalp, and a protruding remnant of skin—part of what used to be an ear.

Tony had been gone from home some three months and had been in so many cities he sometimes woke up in the morning and had no idea where he was. After his arrest, when he learned Chastain was planning another campaign stop in Cleveland, he decided it was a good time to take a break. He decided to return home to be with his family, even if only for a couple of weeks. He told Neary and the group he was not going to travel with them to Chastain's next tour stop in Little Rock, but instead, would catch a bus home. He bummed the fare and promised he would meet up with them in Cleveland.

Rhuloc Futrell was already in Cleveland and Bobby Burk was making arrangements to go.

Crawford

Tony was anxious to return home to his family. He had been a resident of St. Joseph's for months and then "on the campaign trail" for over three months more, eating cold pizza for breakfast and fast food for every other meal and sleeping on floors of apartments belonging to people he had never met...so returning home to his loved ones and his own bed and three squares was heaven. That first Sunday he was home, all of T's brothers and sisters and even Father DiNardo came over after noon Mass to consume Donata's spaghetti and meatball "homecoming dinner" with her "prodigal son." The love and security of his family was just about everything Tony wanted in his life right now; there was only one other thing he felt he had to do and one other place to visit.

The following Monday evening, Tony entered Bobby Lee's gun shop near closing time. The little bell on the door announced his arrival. From the back room someone shouted out, "Be right with you."

Like many first-time visitors to the shop, Tony walked right over to the center display case and picked up the rifle displayed on top, a Remington Arms M24. He placed the stock against his right shoulder and aimed through its scope at one of the trophy bucks hanging high on the wall. He knew this high-powered rifle, or one similar to it, would suit his purposes. He replaced the rifle back in its mount and waited for assistance.

Bobby Lee had already left to spend time with Carrie at St. Joseph's; he entrusted his part-time helper to tend to the shop until his return. The young man eventually came out from the back room and addressed the new customer. "How you doin'? What can I help you with'?"

"In the market for a rifle. I was lookin' at this one right here," pointing to the M24 in the mount on top of the display case.

"That's a terrific weapon but it's kind of pricey."

"Yeah? What am I lookin' at?"

"A little over twelve hundred. But you're a veteran, aren't you?

"Yes."

"Good, because veterans get a significant discount in this shop."

"Really? That's pretty cool."

"The owner sells to veterans at ten percent over cost. Only problem is, you'll have to deal directly with him; he handles all those deals himself and he's not here right now."

"No problem. I understand. I just wanted to check things out today anyway to see what I'm up against. Really not quite ready to buy right now."

"If you want to leave your number, I can have him give you a call."

"No. You know, I'll just come back."

"He opens at ten and he's usually here until about four dependin' on what day it is."

"Okay. I'll just come back. Thanks."

"Thank you."

Tony trundled out of the shop. He knew that even at the discount, it would take him some time to scrape up enough dough to make a purchase.

Two hours later, when Bobby Lee returned from St. Joseph's to close up shop, he asked his clerk how everything went and whether anyone had expressed an interest in the M24.

Cleveland

The Warehouse District, covering eight square blocks close to the center of downtown Cleveland, used to be just that, an area of warehouses. When America used to manufacture things, there was a need for warehouses in cities like Cleveland. The old buildings were now converted into trendy first-floor restaurants, office space, and high-end condominiums and lofts which bordered the surface parking lots. The east end of the district was the location for the county's high-rise Justice Center which housed the courts, the jail, and the Sheriff's Department. It was only a stone's throw from the Cleveland Marriott where Rhuloc Futrell had been employed in housekeeping for the last three weeks.

Chastain's planned second visit to heavily Democratic, blue-collar Cleveland set the city abuzz over the national attention it would receive. Chastain's candidacy was gaining momentum, and his speech in Cleveland would give the city a much-needed opportunity to showcase itself to the nation as well as to remind everyone Chastain was "one of their own." To most of the country, Cleveland was still "The Mistake on the Lake," notwithstanding it had been decades since the heavily-polluted Cuyahoga River last caught fire (that's right...the river actually caught fire on several occasions, the last time in 1969)...followed three years later by the city's mayor using a blow torch in a ribbon-cutting ceremony and accidentally setting fire to his own hair. This was the same mayor whose wife turned down Pat Nixon's invitation to the White House because it was her bowling night. That was "topped" by the infamous "ten-cent beer night" in June of 1974 when the Cleveland Indians, in the midst of a ninth inning comeback, had to forfeit their baseball game to the Texas

Rangers because of a crazed crowd, including a combination of streakers, firecrackers, and stolen bases (literally). Cleveland had been unsuccessfully trying to redeem itself for decades. Perhaps now.

Bobby Lee Burk had travelled to Cleveland from Crawford twice since the campaign's itinerary had been announced. Like Futrell, he studied the how and where of Chastain's last visit to the city, the one Carrie attended. But this time, because of the time of year and the hope for good weather, the speech was planned for an outdoor venue where many more Clevelanders would have the opportunity to see Chastain and listen to his message. It was announced that two huge surface parking lots, surrounded on all four sides by the renovated warehouse buildings, were going to be cleared and a stage set up in the middle. The city had made arrangements to rent the lots for three days and planned to cordon off adjacent streets in order to re-route traffic away from the area. A diagram had been published in *The Plain Dealer* which became a blueprint for the three veterans. The plan was to have the area flooded with people with all eyes focused on the center stage. It was really quite a good plan for the city and would look great on national television, but it was a nightmare for campaign security.

Burk had walked the area several times on each visit to Cleveland. Given his skill and the range of his weapon, he could place himself quite a distance from the temporary stage. It was the great distance, Burk knew, which would make this work. As everyone would have their eyes on Chastain after the fatal shot, no one would think to look as far away as Burk would be. What he found was a six-story parking garage about four blocks to the southeast of "ground zero." On his second visit to the city, he parked within the garage and rode the elevator to the highest parking deck and found an absolutely unobstructed view. He brought with him only the scope off his rifle and was delighted with what he saw as he peered through it. But visiting the roof deck only once was not enough; he had to consider the time of day, the different angles of sunlight and shadows. Four times he ascended to the roof deck of the parking garage, and each time he grew more confident. His preliminary plan was to arrive the day before the speech to ensure a ground floor parking space within the garage, ascend to the top deck, finish his business, leave the rifle, and exit the garage driving east, away from the cordoned-off Warehouse District. I-90 was only seven blocks away. He timed the route. If he caught all the lights, he could be on the interstate within eight minutes of squeezing off the fatal round, and before anyone even looked in the direction of the parking garage.

Rhuloc Futrell had already completed step one of his plan; he was hired at the Marriott, the downtown hotel closest to the site of the speech. Not wanting to make the same mistakes as Lee Harvey, he was prepared to keep the housekeeping job for at least six weeks following Chastain's death. Unlike Burk, there was no need to arrange a quick getaway. The beauty of Futrell's scheme was he would be "invisible in plain sight," just another one of the masses, spending his lunch break to hear Chastain. Like Burk, however, he figured a long-range, high-powered rifle was the way to go.

He overpaid by the week for a one-room efficiency in a warehouse building not yet renovated; one of those deals where the owners were investing nothing in the place, waiting for the downtown housing market to "creep" close enough in their direction to justify a major financial outlay. The building was six stories tall and sat four blocks to the southwest, kitty-corner from the spot Chastain's podium would ultimately be placed. The shot from its roof would be very challenging but that was the beauty of it. Rhuloc figured law enforcement would consider a shot from that direction, that far down the street, at that angle, to be simply too difficult and highly unlikely. But he remained confident he could pull it off.

The roof of the building featured a three-foot stone/brick parapet wall which was crumbling. It was a perfect cover. Futrell planned to leave the Marriott, return to his apartment, take the old stairwell up to the roof, do the deed, stash the weapon, and sneak into the pandemonium which would then be escalating on the ground.

Chastain Comes to Cleveland

When the day finally arrived a week later, Tony Icovatti had made arrangements to meet his group at the Greyhound station which was just east of the rally site. From there, the veterans walked the few blocks to the already-congested spot, arriving about thirty minutes before Chastain's campaign bus—"Carrie Burk's bus." They quickly surveyed the area. The best station for their protest happened to be in the same direction as Futrell's "flophouse." A restored warehouse building across the street from the temporary stage housed a legal clinic and had four courses of sandstone steps leading up to its newly designed entrance. Neary decided right in front of the entrance would be a good vantage point for them and their bullhorns; it was a bit elevated and would probably get them some TV time—their ultimate goal.

A half hour later, the group, minus Tony Icovatti, could see the bus making its way toward the stage, slowly parting the crowd before it like Moses parted the Red Sea. When its doors opened and Chastain came into sight, the crowd went nuts. Security tried to clear a path to the stage, but it became more like a gauntlet, everyone sticking out their hands and Chastain shaking hands with everyone as he went.

He ascended the steps and was met by every Democrat office holder in Northern Ohio, the ones who pulled every string they could to get on the stage and get "face time" with the candidate. A picture with Chastain, they hoped, would further their own campaigns, believing his coattails would be easy to ride. He stepped up to the microphone, but it was almost ten minutes before the crowd was quiet enough for Chastain to be heard.

Tony wondered to himself how the man could possibly receive such a reception when he had done absolutely nothing to deserve it.

Chastain started out well, "Thank you. Thank you so much. Thank you, Cleveland...my hometown." The crowd went crazy and another five minutes had to pass.

"You know, I told the driver to take me to the Dawg Pound but he took me here instead." The crowd was delirious. More waiting.

After thanking the mayor and a host of other Democrats, he launched into his address. "Ladies and gentlemen, our nation stands at a crossroads. The decisions this country will make over the next fourteen months will set our nation's course for generations to come. We need to re-examine our priorities and re-direct our country's resources.

"We have too many men of science, too few men of God. We have grasped the mystery of the atom and rejected the Sermon on the Mount. The world has achieved brilliance without wisdom, power without conscience. Ours is a world of nuclear giants and ethical infants. We know more about war than we know about peace, more about killing than we know about living."

"Friends, these words are not my words. General Omar Bradley spoke them over sixty years ago, but they remain true today. It is now up to our generation, a new generation, to conduct our affairs with both wisdom and conscience, to learn how to live in peace...and to embrace the Sermon on the Mount. Blessed are the peacemakers for they shall be called the children of God. Let us be the peacemakers."

"Friends, we enjoy the greatest democracy the world has ever known, but know this: Democracy cannot be forced upon all the countries of our world. It cannot be imposed upon societies whose religions, cultures and values have no relationship to our own. We have no right to meddle in the internal affairs of these nations regardless of how we may abhor their politics. Until we learn this lesson, we will be condemned to repeat the failures of Korea, Vietnam, Iraq, and Afghanistan. Make no mistake, we were not defending our democracy in those foreign lands; we were trying to impose it upon cultures incapable of accepting it!"

The single shot rang out as he paused to sip his water. The back of his head exploded like a pumpkin smashed by a Louisville slugger. The brain that conceived his politics was now splattered like curdled strawberry yogurt over both Teleprompters. In that same instant, one gunman had taken aim through his high-powered scope and had the clearest view of the fatal shot but had no idea where it came from. The other gunman smiled and quickly left his post. Tony Icovatti froze, experiencing a ghastly flashback that would haunt him the remainder of his life.

Blood, hair, chunks of brain tissue, and parts of Chastain's skull flew into the crowd. People were running in every direction but mostly into each other. The Democrats were jumping off the stage to get as far away from Chastain as quickly as possible. His lifeless body fell forward into the podium and rode it down as it fell off the front of the stage. He came to rest face down on top of it, exposing the grotesque mess that used to be the back of his head. The cameras there to record Chastain's speech were instead capturing the chaos.

The FBI agents who had been tracking Neary had him and his small group rounded up within a half hour; camo might work well in the desert, but it had a reverse effect in downtown Cleveland. Nevertheless, it took a while before they could apprehend Tony amid the pandemonium; he had not been with the group. Rhuloc Futrell had already descended from his roost to "melt" into the mayhem as was his plan, and Burk was westbound on Interstate 90 on his way out of the city. Futrell ended up standing very close by as the agents finally found Icovatti, surrounded him, and took him into custody while cameras flashed and the videos continued to roll. The image of the agents surrounding Tony as Futrell and others looked on was only one among thousands recorded that day, but within the week would appear on the front page in every newspaper in the world...and define the event.

Harley Daull and Chester Mylott watched on the big screen in the Vice Presidential library as all the national networks broke away from regularly scheduled programming to provide live streaming of the events following the fatal shot. One particular video of Chastain as he took the bullet was preceded with a cautionary note regarding its graphic nature.

Marie Patronite was in her car returning from a visit with her mother when the news came across the radio. She had grossly miscalculated. She didn't think Daull would act so quickly; she thought she had more time. She pulled onto the berm of the Expressway to calm herself.

The band of veterans, including Tony, was transported by van the very short distance to the Justice Center where they were separately interrogated by agents of the Federal Bureau of Investigation with the assistance of two sheriff's detectives. Another Deputy Sheriff was listing all the news agencies and television stations there to report on the rally. Neary's group was detained for almost a day and a half until "everything was sorted out," copies of the videos were scrutinized, and the agents felt confident the protestors, including Tony, had nothing to do with the assassination.

Crawford

One week later, three FBI agents traveled to Crawford to arrest Tony for the murder of Alexander Chastain. They advised him of his right to remain silent but they really didn't need to; he had been incapable of coherent speech since he saw Chastain's head explode. Following his arrest, every newspaper in the United States carried the image on their front page of Tony in Cleveland being surrounded by the FBI agents, the one with Futrell and others standing right there watching. They reported a high-powered sniper rifle which the FBI suspected was the murder weapon had been found, a rifle which had Tony Icovatti's fingerprints on it, and was reportedly stolen from a gun shop in Tony's hometown. They also shared information regarding the activities of Neary's group for the six months leading up to the Cleveland rally. Some of the papers included a picture of a distraught Tony right after his arrest. He hadn't slept since returning from Cleveland. He had bloodshot eyes; ragged, unkempt hair; reddened, jagged scalp; and a hideous piece of left ear. Everyone reading the accounts and viewing the pictures was sure Icovatti was another disgruntled, deranged veteran—another Timothy McVeigh. Everyone, that is, except Marie Patronite. When she read the accounts and saw the picture of Icovatti, with Futrell in the midst of the melee, she was certain how it all came about.

Despite his meticulous planning, Bobby Lee Burk had screwed up. Three days before he left for the Chastain rally in Cleveland, he had used a crowbar to pry open the rear door to his shop so the next morning he could report a break-in to the Crawford Police. They investigated the "crime" and learned from Burk a Remington M24 sniper rifle had been stolen. The investigating officers knew Bobby Lee very well and they had absolutely no reason to doubt him. Bobby Lee thought he had it perfectly set up: The weapon had been stolen from his shop three days before Chastain's assassination, a weapon Burk was careful not to leave any fingerprints on. What he didn't know...until he read the newspaper accounts like everyone else...was that Tony Icovatti had.

Tony was in another place; he had no concept for what was happening to him or why. True, he had given some consideration to taking Chastain out, but in the end, he found neither the will nor the wherewithal to accomplish it. When he saw what happened to Chastain, he didn't see Chastain. He was delivered back to Sadr City where he saw the horrific, frozen dead stare of Sally...in a helmet bouncing away from him across the rubble left by the IED.

Backward little Crawford was buzzing with the news of Tony's arrest and everything being reported in the national news. People, some with little or no real information and most with loads of misinformation, immediately formed their opinions and took up sides. *There is no way this boy could have done it; he came from a good family and was a decorated war hero who paid dearly for his service to his country.* That group was countered by others. *The poor kid lost his mind; he had stalked the senator for months until he got his chance—and he took it.* Crawford Attorney Ted Chase read the accounts and watched the national news just like everyone else. Mac, his mentor, taught him never to assume anything, and that lesson was reinforced over and over again during Ted's years of trial work. He had recently concluded the defense of two men charged with the murder of a local chiropractor, a seemingly "open-and-shut case," which was anything but open and shut. He had many discussions at dinner with Dorie and the kids as developments unfolded in the national media. He wondered, given what he had learned thus far, when some "high-profile" lawyer (the media always described the lawyer that way no matter who it was) would be brought in to defend the young man. CNN had already unleashed their "talking heads," who, at this early stage, added nothing but conjecture and confusion and irresponsibly so: They were immediately quoted and misquoted by folks trying to show off how much they knew.

Three days later, Bettino and Donata Icovatti were in his office.

The Prosecutor's Office in Cleveland

Forty-six-year-old J. Michael Gerrity was winding down his second term as the Cuyahoga County Prosecutor. Long ago, he had decided to leave the daily courtroom "grind" to his "minions." He had not tried a case in over six years. But that did not mean he didn't put himself "out front" for every "high-profile" case in his office. Regardless of which assistant prosecutor received the trial assignment, Northern Ohioans would see only the face of J. Michael on their television sets and read quotes only from him in their newspapers. He was the consummate politician who kept a tight rein on his office and all those who worked for him. He had started "in the trenches" of the Democratic Party as a very young man and had worked his way to its pinnacle; he "controlled" the Party in Northern Ohio.

For the six months leading up to Chastain's murder, Gerrity had been laying the groundwork for his campaign for the governorship. He knew he had an uphill battle because of the deep and widespread disdain for Cuyahoga County and its politicians held by his contemporaries to the south. They continued to regard Cleveland as "the mistake on the lake" and on statewide matters, they seldom, if ever voted for measures or candidates from the city to the north. Support for a Gerrity run at the governor's office was largely non-existent south of Route 30. He desperately needed to enhance his name recognition in the southern part of the State and "get the message out" that even though he was a Democrat, he was a somewhat conservative "law and order" guy who steadfastly believed in the Second Amendment.

What a stroke of luck! Chastain was assassinated in Cleveland! The timing could not have been better! Vincent Bugliosi and others like him had enjoyed significant political as well as financial success following a triumphant high-profile prosecution. Some, like Marsha Clark, had even prospered after abject failure! Why not him? One book alone could be worth hundreds of thousands to him...but the political value would be priceless. Within three hours of Chastain's gruesome death, the sheriff and Gerrity appeared on every national evening newscast providing details about their investigation already underway.

Two days later, the most junior assistant county prosecutor was called to Gerrity's office to report on the "emergency" research assignment he had been given. It was the young lawyer's first "one-on-one" with Gerrity and he was plenty nervous. Gerrity shook his hand.

"Kurland, is it?"

"Yes, sir. Jim."

"What have you got for me, Jim?"

"The Code of Federal Regulations states the murder of a member of Congress or a major presidential or vice presidential candidate shall be punishable by imprisonment for any term of years including for life—or by death. A major presidential or vice-presidential candidate is defined in Section 3056 of the CFR."

"I assume Chastain fits within the Code two different ways then?"

"Yes, sir, he did. Violation of this section of the CFR is to be investigated by the Federal Bureau of Investigation who may, at their discretion, call upon local authorities for their assistance."

"What about jurisdiction?"

"Jurisdiction is concurrent."

"So the county can assert jurisdiction to prosecute?"

"It can. However, Subsection (f) states if Federal prosecutive jurisdiction is asserted for violation of this section of the CFR, that assertion shall suspend the jurisdiction exercised by the State or local authority."

"So the Feds can trump us?"

"Yes, sir. It appears that way."

"Good job, Jim. Write it up and have it on my desk by the end of the day. Good job."

"Yes, sir. Thank you, sir."

Gerrity had to quickly formulate a plan because he was now in a race with the Federal District Attorney for the Northern District of Ohio. Gerrity's goal was to "steal" the case right from under the nose of the Feds, get a conviction while the entire nation watched and then "waltz" into the governor's office—all before reaching age fifty. He had a lot of political "chits" out there and he immediately started to work the phone to call them in. He wanted this prosecution more than anything else in the world, but it had nothing to do with seeing justice done for Alexander Chastain. The first call he made was to Chester Mylott.

The Law Offices of Rosenthall Chase

"Jenny, please put the Icovattis in the library. Make them as comfortable as you can and tell them I will be right with them. Then please get Mac on the line for me."

Bettino and Donata Icovatti were content to lead what most would consider "small" lives on their farm in rural Crawford County, which they seldom left. Their children and grandchild were their existence, and other than the congregation of St. Rocco's Parish, they rarely needed anyone else or anything more. Their lives were shaped by the events in the lives of their children: new arrivals, birthday celebrations, holidays and holy days, spelling bees, basketball games, school dances, "Church doings," showers, and graduations. The needs of the family also dictated their needs. Their son's ordeal, however, took them away from their "sanctuary" and forced them into foreign places: Walter Reed Hospital, the office of a psychiatrist within the innards of St. Joseph's, Cleveland's Justice Center which Bettino described as like "being inside a huge public toilet," and now the law office of a criminal defense lawyer. They felt like "aliens" in these unfamiliar places as they sat quietly waiting to meet "Mr. Attorney Chase."

Ted wanted to speak with his mentor and former trial practice professor, James McIlvaine before meeting with the Icovattis.

"Mac, Ted."

"Theodore, how's everyone?"

"Fine, Mac."

"And the in-laws?"

"Fine, too."

"What's up?"

"Mac, I need your help."

"Oh?"

"Corporal Anthony Icovatti's parents are in my library."

Silence.

"Mac, I know what they want, and I am not sure I can do it."

Silence.

"Not sure I can expose myself to that level of scrutiny and the firm...and my family. Jesus Christ."

"Ted, why don't you speak with them but don't make any commitments just yet. How about I come over to the house this evening?"

"Can you? God, oh that would be great, Mac. Jesus."

"Ted, I'll be there for dinner. Tell Dorie that chicken dish she makes will do just fine." Mac was a longtime widower playfully "in love" with Ted's wife, Dorie.

"Sure...chicken. Thanks, Mac. See you around six."

"See you then. And...oh...Ted, Optimus Prime was right."

"Optimus Prime? The transformer? What the hell does that mean?"

"Fate rarely calls upon us at a moment of our choosing."

"Yeah...right. Jesus Christ."

He hung up but he didn't move; he just sat there. A shiver passed through his body. After five minutes, he gathered enough courage to meet Tony's parents. The two of them were "train wrecks." Donata held her small handkerchief in her left hand and covered her puffy eyes with her right as she stared down at the library's conference table. Bettino was sitting next to her staring blankly forward. Even after Ted entered the room, it took Bettino several seconds to react. He tried to get to his feet as soon as he possibly could but Ted stretched out his arm and said, "No, no...please sit. Please sit."

Ted extended his hand to Bettino who took it in his meaty, calloused, farmer's hand and they shook. He then took Donata's petite, weak, still moist hand.

"Welcome. Can I get either of you something to drink?"

"No, thank you. They already asked."

"I understand you would like to speak with me about representing your son."

"Yes." Bettino took the lead in the conversation.

"Have you been to see him?"

"Yes, yesterday in Cleveland. He is not well. We tried to speak with him, but he couldn't talk with us; he was making no sense. It is the worst he's been since he got back."

"From the Middle East."

"Yes, from the Middle East. He stayed with us for a while and then at St. Joseph's for several months before he went on the road."

"He was at St. Joseph's?"

Donata looked up. "Yes."

"So he was having some problems when he returned from the service?"

"Yes. Major depression and post-traumatic stress disorder. His best friend was killed by a roadside bomb and he was severely injured."

"The Colonna boy."

"Yes."

"Can I ask why you want me?"

"We read the papers, Mr. Chase. You had a couple of cases the papers reported on and we wanted someone close to home."

"I see."

"We can afford to pay you."

One of the problems with the law is the discussion of fees usually came at a time when the client was most in need, most vulnerable and many attorneys took advantage. The problem here was this case would certainly take up six months of the coming year, six months when Ted would be able to devote little, if any, time to other client matters. And it wouldn't only be Ted; his paralegal Mike would also be making a huge commitment of his time, and also Mac, who Ted would have sit second chair. There were other considerations as well. His every decision, every move would be second-guessed by the television talking heads from the comfort of the sidelines. This amount of stress on Ted and his firm as it was exposed to the world (and how it may affect their families) had to be weighed before a decision to undertake the client. What Ted recognized deep down inside, and what he feared, was he and his firm would, for all time, be measured by the outcome of this singular case. It could be incredibly beneficial...or it could be an utter disaster, but he recognized those as selfish considerations.

"Tony is innocent; he couldn't have done anything like that," Donata announced.

But what about his state of mind? A mental capacity defense could certainly be in play here, Ted thought to himself. "Tell me, who was taking care of Tony at St. Joseph's?"

"Dr. Berringer."

"I understand your son attended several of the Chastain rallies."

"That's right. He left St. Joseph's and met up with some other vets and they went to the rallies. He would call us from time to time to let us know where he was and that he was alright. Was gone for about three months. He came home for a couple weeks before he went to Cleveland. Seemed absolutely fine then. But Sally's death hit him hard; really, really hard. They were so close."

"Sally?"

"The Colonna boy. Name was Salvatore, but T called him Sally."

"Oh, I see. Look, what I really need to do is discuss the matter with my partners because there are a lot of considerations. I would have to devote almost one hundred percent of my time to the defense of your son, and that would mean my partners would have to step up to take care of other matters I would normally handle. For a case of this magnitude, I am certain it would be about a six-month commitment. The case would have to be tried in Cleveland which is another consideration. Before we talk too much more about Tony and all that went on, let me talk it over with my partners tomorrow and then we can meet again. Is that okay? I should be able to get back with you within two days."

Bettino slowly arose, "Thank you, Mr. Chase. I will pray that you will help us." Donata said nothing but the look on her face said everything. Ted couldn't begin to fathom what she had been through; her son coming home in pieces—with demons—and now being compared to Sirhan Sirhan, Lee Harvey Oswald, and Tim McVeigh.

Ted escorted them out and then sat back down, staring at the wall of books. Like just about every other practitioner who went out on his own or started his own firm, Ted's collection of law books and reference materials began with his law school texts. There was a small, corner section of the library where Ted and his partners shelved theirs. Ted walked over, bent down, and retrieved his Criminal Law book which probably had not been off a shelf in twenty years. He opened it to the chapters devoted to the defense of mental insanity. There were long discussions of the M'Naghten rule, "irresistible impulse," Durham aka "the product rule," and the Model Penal Code, different judicial theories addressing the defense of mental incompetence. The fact such a list even existed was proof our country's jurisprudence had really not figured it out; the standard applied to this type of criminal conduct varied from jurisdiction to jurisdiction. Few doctrines in criminal law had generated more controversy than the insanity defense. It seems our society has yet to decide what the proper relationship should be between mental disease and criminal responsibility. On one hand, the criminal defendant's heinous crime shocks the community and screams out for retribution, but on the other, there remains a root belief it is wrong to punish an individual who is seriously mentally ill. The fact that we do not blame an insane individual justifies in us holding the sane defendant guilty. We identify the distinction between those who are mad and those who are bad, between those who can control their conduct and those who cannot. The other major problem is the defense presents the confluence of psychiatry and law, two disciplines which rarely, if ever, "speak the same language."

There are really two considerations. The first is the defendant's competency to stand trial which is decided by the judge rather than the jury. Most states, including Ohio, have laws on the books prohibiting the trial of an incompetent defendant; the individual lacks the capacity to aid in his defense or meaningfully confront his accusers, both basic rights guaranteed by our Constitution. Additionally, the whole reason for the prosecution is called into doubt: retribution and deterrence mean nothing to a mentally incompetent defendant. Should the trial go forward, the second, larger issue is for the jury to decide: What was the defendant's mental state when he did the deed? At the time of the conduct, did the defendant have the capacity to know right from wrong or was he robbed of this by mental disease? When confronted with the decision whether or not to "plead insanity," almost all attorneys would enter two pleas on behalf of their client: Not

Guilty and Not Guilty by Reason of Insanity. By proceeding in that manner, they maintained all their legal options.

He closed the book and made a mental note to ask Mike, his paralegal, to draft a short memo on the current state of the insanity defense in Ohio. He will ask him to research the most recent Ohio Supreme Court pronouncements on the issue and also those decisions emanating from Ohio's several appellate districts. He was particularly interested in decisions coming out of the Eighth Appellate District, Cuyahoga County, where Chastain had been murdered.

Mac

Ted's father passed away a broken man, very young, during Ted's third year of law school and there were some men who helped fill the void. One was his father-in-law, Jack, and the other was James McIlvaine, his trial practice instructor who was now retired. Early on, Mac had recognized a special talent in young Ted and he helped him to cultivate it. Even now, so many years after graduation, they remained close. When Ted began his new firm, Rosenthall Chase, Mac was on the letterhead as "Of Counsel."

Mac, now in his early seventies, lost his beloved Patty to breast cancer years before he and Ted met. Mac was so devoted to her, and he had vowed no one could ever take her place; he had been on his own for over twenty-five years. After Ted introduced Mac to Dorie, his fiancé, a special relationship between the three grew. Mac routinely professed his "undying love" for Dorie and warned Ted he would, someday, steal her away, notwithstanding he was old enough to be her father. And Dorie always played along. They made a point to "flirt" with each other in front of Ted and take swipes at him in the process. More than once,

Ted had referred to Mac as "an old pervert," and Mac, just as often, would smilingly agree. After graduation, Ted found himself seeking Mac's advice often and not only about the law. Mac was happily entrenched as a very important member of the Chase family.

Mac arrived for his favorite chicken dinner a little after six. Given the topic of discussion for the evening, dinner was only for three. The kids had been sent to Dorie's parents. Dorie met him at the door.

Taking Dorie in his arms theatrically, "Ah...my beautiful princess. Are you ready to escape this dastardly ogre and fly away with me to the island of unending love?"

Glancing back at Ted who was standing immediately behind her, she didn't miss a beat, "Yes, my fair prince. I have eagerly awaited your rescue."

"Sheesh, I have never heard anyone spew more bullshit...even for an Irishman."

They all laughed as Mac planted a big kiss on Dorie.

"And do I smell Chicken Kelly straight from the oven?"

"You do."

Pointing at Ted, "My God, if it weren't for this third wheel here, I would think I am in heaven."

They laughed some more.

Mac sat at the dining room table as Dorie brought out the main dish, followed by the mashed potatoes and carrot casserole with celery and breadcrumbs on top. Ted brought out a cold bottle of Keystone Light and poured Mac a glass.

Mac said, "What is this pig swill?"

"We save the Guinness for the important guests."

"I often wonder how I ever made the mistake of giving you a passing grade."

"It was just like everything else you did. You screwed up."

They laughed.

The dinner conversation was mostly about the kids who Mac treated like grandchildren. Most of that conversation focused upon Ted's oldest daughter who had just decided boys were not such a bad thing after all...and all the ramifications that come along with that discovery.

Over a dessert of homemade apple pie and piping hot black coffee, the discussion turned to Tony Icovatti.

"So, Ted, you have had some time to consider this. What are you thinking?"

"Still not sure. You know I have done NGRI work before; it's not that. I'm just not sure I'm ready for the exposure: all the media attention and other baggage that comes with it. And it's not just me; the firm will be under the microscope and I'm uncertain how all our families will deal with all of this. It just seems too big right now."

"Did the parents say why they picked you?"

"They wanted someone from Crawford. They had read the papers about the *Giffen* trial and Tehan."

"Case will be tried in Cleveland."

"Yeah, that's a whole 'nother can of worms."

"It will be televised every day."

"Don't doubt it. Mac, from what I know so far, it will be an incredibly hard case for us to make."

"I understand, but maybe that's not such a bad thing either. I'm thinking the expectations of an acquittal or even getting him off on a NGRI will be pretty low. It's like right now we've got nowhere to go but up. What do you think, Dorie?"

"I just want to be sure that everyone is safe while all this is going on. There are so many nut cases out there," her voice trailed off.

That was a point neither Ted nor Mac had considered.

Ted said, "And what about the financial end of it? I mean how do we begin to gauge the amount of time we'll have to invest? Certainly, I'll need to be devoted to it one hundred percent, and I would want you second chair so there would be your time and Mike's as well. And trial in Cleveland—that means extended stays during the week for as long as it takes. And let's not forget the experts we'll need, certainly a psychiatrist and perhaps a ballistics expert. Between fees and expenses, we'll get to six figures in a heartbeat, I'm sure. You know the Icovattis said they could afford to pay, but I'm sure they have no idea what's really involved here."

"In all honesty Ted, I don't think we can evaluate this case like other criminal matters the firm has handled. Most likely, whatever the Icovattis are capable of putting up will be devoured by the costs alone. We may end up working for pennies an hour but I'll argue it is still a case we should handle. I know of similar situations where the collateral benefits far exceeded any hourly fee."

"Collateral benefits?"

"If you take the case, in the public's eyes you will be moving to a whole different level. We're talking 'Dream Team,' F. Lee...that sort of thing. Johnny Cochran was a fine lawyer but no one outside of LA knew much about him until the OJ prosecution."

"Mac, this isn't LA. We're a small law firm in small Crawford, Ohio. I'm not sure how high a profile we want to have. We've been doing very well just the way we are. And what if it ends in a crushing defeat? What kind of 'collateral benefit' would that leave us with? Everyone thinking we were in over our heads from the get-go? Our inflated egos wouldn't let us pass up the case?"

"Ted, you know deep down you're ready for this. The 'stage' may be a bit different, larger—but I have been right with you for all these years and have seen you work. Cochran, rest his soul, on his best day had nothin' on you. I'm not just saying that. I don't believe the Icovattis could make a better choice. More importantly, let's not forget what's on the line here or forget the oath we took when we were sworn in as lawyers. We may not hit a home run with an acquittal, but we may be able to save this young man's life. I think we should do it. You should certainly talk it over with the other partners, and if they have no strong objections, I think we should take the case."

"Well, Mac...why don't we hear what they have to say. They will be doing double duty if you and I get tied up with this thing. We're talking months."

"I'm sure."

Number One, Observatory Circle

Harley Daull was scheduled to address a group of United Auto Workers at a Pennsylvania parts plant the next afternoon and he and Mylott were in Daull's library working on his speech. He clicked off the big screen after the evening's newscast, looked at his right-hand man with utter disbelief, and asked, "Who the hell is Anthony Icovatti?"

Mylott responded, "From what I've learned so far, he's a disgruntled vet whose fingerprints were found on the rifle. Badly hurt in Iraq, had some problems. Had a hard-on for Chastain. He was following him around."

"Our guy takes Chastain out, but the rifle has someone else's prints on it? How does that happen?"

"Don't know how he pulled it off but that's the only thing I could figure. I told you; Futrell is sharp."

"Did you settle up with him?"

"Yes."

"Did he let on about any of this?"

"Didn't talk with him. Figured out a way to get the money to him without a meeting. Harley, looks like we've got nothing to worry about here. Sounds to me this Icovatti fellow is in a world of shit though."

"Our guy was good enough to get the job done and implicate someone else in the process?"

"I guess so. Looks that way."

"Jeeeeesuuuss Christ. What's Icovatti lookin' at? It's a capital crime, isn't it?"

"Death is one sentencing option. Could be life or even something less. Harley, there's one other thing."

"Oh?"

"Our guy in Cleveland, Gerrity, desperately wants this prosecution. He's already called."

"Mike Gerrity?"

"Yes."

"But it's Federal, isn't it?"

"Only if the Feds take it. Gerrity wants us to keep the Feds out of it."

"What's his agenda?"

"The governorship which isn't a bad thing for us either. Might go a long way for us taking Ohio. Think it through; we get him the prosecution and he owes us. Plus...he gets this Icovatti nutcase convicted and no one is the wiser. It's better than 'plausible deniability.' Harley, it will never get back to us. Actually...it comes together rather well for everyone."

"It doesn't come out too well for Icovatti."

"In military jargon, I think that's called collateral damage."

"What do we do with the District Attorney? He'll want the case, won't he?"

"That's the easy part. We offer him a high-profile job in the new administration, something he can't pass up."

Daull was now staring out the window trying to think everything through. He finally said, "Let's go ahead and make the calls. I'll want to talk with both men. Start with the District Attorney. We'll need him on board first and then I'll go to bat for Gerrity and see if can get him the case. I'll think of something. But Gerrity's got to understand...I don't want Icovatti 'takin' the needle' on this, Chester. No matter what happens, Icovatti does not get the death sentence. If Gerrity doesn't agree to that, I'll make sure he doesn't get the prosecution."

Step one of Daull's "grand scheme" was now complete; it was time for him to move on to the second part of the plan. He had recognized the appeal of Chastain's politics and now that Chastain was "removed," Daull intended to take up his message and put the nomination to bed. The remaining candidates were weak: a longer-than-long-shot, big-mouthed Congressman from Ohio and a little-known, first-term Midwestern governor with an ego bigger than his State. Step two would begin tomorrow with Daull's speech. He intended to use several quotes from JFK's June 1963 American University commencement address in his remarks to the Auto Workers.

Most Americans believed Kennedy's most compelling speech was his inaugural address which implored every American to "Ask not what your country can do for you, ask what you can do for your country." Those who studied the Cold War and Kennedy's role in it would strongly disagree. Kennedy's remarks to the graduating class of American University in 1963, just months before his death, were designed by him to send a loud and clear message to the enemies of the United States. His goal was to put an end to the Cold War and seek a peace; however not a "pax Americana" forced upon the world by America's bullying and weapons of war, but a "genuine peace, not merely a peace in our time but peace for all time."

Chastain had believed Kennedy's words were even more relevant now. Speaking of (but really to) America's Cold War enemies during his 1963 commencement address, Kennedy had extended an olive branch:

> "So, let us not be blind to our differences—but let us also direct attention to our common interests and the means by which those differences can be resolved. And if we cannot end now our differences, at least we can help make the world safe for diversity. For, in the final analysis, our most basic common link is that we all inhabit this small planet. We all breathe the same air. We all cherish our children's futures. And we are all mortal."

Kennedy had made it clear: his new agenda for the country, regardless of its military who clamored for war, was to "make the world safe for diversity," not democracy. He wanted a real peace, not a "pax Americana" America could impose only by flexing its muscle. He continued:

> "Never before has man had such capacity to control his own environment, to end thirst and hunger, to conquer poverty and disease, to banish illiteracy and massive human misery. We have the power to make

> this the best generation of mankind in the history of the world or to make it the last."

History has shown Kennedy's 1963 commencement address at American University was immediately scrutinized and analyzed by Nikita Krushev and his political strategists. History has also shown, in the entire world, the two men most disheartened by Kennedy's assassination were Krushev and Fidel Castro for they realized an opportunity for a "real" peace died along with him.

Chastain, for all his faults, clearly recognized nothing had changed since the 1960s; decades after Kennedy's murder, we had learned nothing. Few Americans understood the "military-industrial complex" President Eisenhower had warned us about in 1959 had come to fruition...and continues to this day to be the most powerful political force within our country. Kennedy was murdered in November of 1963, literally weeks after he had decided to withdraw all U.S. military forces from Vietnam. (There were only thirty-five hundred "advisors" in Vietnam at that time.) Because of his death, the plan to withdraw turned instead into escalation at the urging of the CIA and the Pentagon...and utter defeat. Three bullets from an assassin's cheap Italian rifle were a death sentence, not only for a President, but also for fifty-eight thousand Americans...whose only legacy was to have their names engraved on a stone wall in Washington...not far from Kennedy's eternal flame. Their comrades, the lucky ones who survived the debacle of Vietnam, returned to a thankless nation.

While Daull and Mylott were trying to figure things out, Rhuloc Futrell had just started his evening shift at the Cleveland Marriot. A package had arrived that day by messenger and Futrell had it well hidden in the room he rented by the week. He thought he would stay in Cleveland for about two more weeks and then leave for home with his newfound wealth. What had really happened the day Chastain died, well he wasn't about to figure it out and, more importantly, there was no need. If this Mylott moron wanted to pay him one hundred "big ones" for Chastain's life, that was his business. Other than disrupting his own life for a couple months, Futrell had done nothing to earn the money. Through the telescopic lens of his rifle, he had the best view of anyone in Cleveland of the back of Chastain's head when it exploded, but who pulled that off, he had no clue.

After thinking it through, he realized Mylott would certainly believe he had delivered. Futrell's goal had been to get the balance of his "fee" as quickly as possible and disappear before Mylott, or whoever he was working for, stumbled across the truth. It was the easiest one hundred grand anyone could ever earn. If Mylott had any questions for him when they "settled up," Futrell intended to lie his ass off. Turns out, Mylott figured out a way for him to get his money without even talking with him; Futrell was "home free."

St. Joseph's

Ted Chase and Dr. Michael Berringer had previously collaborated on the Laurie Giffen matter and were friends. The doctor met Ted at the door to his office.

"Ted, how have you been?"

"Fine, Doc, and you?"

"I've been well Ted...busy. How's the family?"

"Fine, thanks."

"And Mac?"

"Still a stubborn old coot."

"So he is well then," laughing.

"Yeah, he's fine."

"So...you're really swimming among the alligators now," with a smile on his face.

"Looks that way."

They moved over to the overstuffed furniture which surrounded the doctor's coffee table which already held a tray with a fresh pot of coffee. Berringer poured two cups. "Just black, isn't it?"

"Good memory."

"So, I understand you want to talk further with Tony today."

"Yes."

"We were absolutely astounded you persuaded the court in Cleveland to allow Tony to stay here while he was awaiting trial."

"How many agents are here?"

"There is a contingent of twelve in shifts around the clock, all plain-clothed. One is stationed at the door of his room, one in the lobby and two in separate cars in our parking lots, one in front and one in back. No one gets in and out of here without their consent. They're monitoring Tony with an ankle bracelet."

"How is he?"

"Not good. You will have a hard time getting anything out of him. Since his arraignment, he has basically 'shut down.' Barely communicates at all. We can sometimes get a phrase or two out of him—kind of goes in and out. Any progress we had made before he left here has been wiped out; he has regressed...perhaps to a state even worse than when he first arrived. We really have to do everything for him now, make sure he gets showered, shaved...everything."

"And this was all just because he was arrested?"

"No, much more than that. Hard to tell. We don't know what went on during the three months or so after he left here or what happened to him in Cleveland."

"Doc, can you sit in with me?"

"Sure, if you think it would help."

"Where should we do it?"

"Actually, right here would be best; it is usually where he and I meet and he has somewhat of a comfort level. We should make it appear we are just having a conversation. What are you after?"

"I think basically the same thing you are. I would like to know what went on while he was following Chastain around and what happened in Cleveland. When he joined the group of veterans, he caught the attention of the FBI. They assembled a file on him which I've already seen. The weapon they suspect fired the shot has Tony's fingerprints on it. If we're 'dead to rights' on the 'Not Guilty,' we may have to go strictly the 'Insanity' route."

Ted was hoping for an immediate acknowledgement from the doctor at this last statement but received none. Both men realized the doctor's opinion on the issue could either make or break the defense, but the doctor knew not to make any representations at this time.

Ten minutes later, Tony joined them, having been "escorted" to Berringer's office. Ted could tell by the way he looked and what he was wearing he was being taken care of. It was as if he were an eight-year-old whose mother dressed him and then had to plead with him to comb his hair and brush his teeth. There was no emotion, just a blank stare.

Dr. Berringer poured Tony a glass of ice water and placed it on the table in front of him. "Tony, you already know Ted here. He was with you in Cleveland...in court for the arraignment."

The corporal looked over toward Ted but offered no response, no acknowledgement they had ever met before.

"Ted and I wanted to go over some things with you."

Nothing.

Berringer glanced over to Ted and then Ted, in a soft voice, asked, "Tony, what can you tell me about Alexander Chastain?"

Almost like flipping a switch, the 'lights went on' and an answer came out, "He raped Carrie."

What?!

Ted had no idea what that meant, and he looked over at the doctor who had almost fallen out of his chair. Berringer immediately raised his hand to Ted...like a stop sign, but that direction was unnecessary; in an instant Ted knew he had to get out of the way of this conversation. *What in the hell?!*

Berringer took over. "Tony, what did you say?"

"Chastain raped Carrie."

"Carrie Burk?"

"Yes, on the bus."

"Bus?"

"His campaign bus."

"How do you know this?"

"Carrie."

"Carrie told you?"

"Yes."

"Tony, she hasn't spoken to us since she's been here."

"So?"

"You're saying Carrie Burk spoke with you and told you she was raped by Senator Chastain when she was on his bus?"

"Yes, and some other men too."

Berringer looked at Ted. "I am sorry, Ted, but you'll have to come back another day."

Ted fully understood and he nodded as he got up to leave.

He could hardly concentrate on his driving. Ted knew only what the local paper had reported about Carrie Burk. She was repeatedly described as "the wife of a local gun shop owner" but Ted had never met the husband. He knew her case was still "under investigation" and presently there were more questions than there were answers. He also had no idea Carrie had been a resident of St. Joseph's. Now, Ted's client, on trial for the assassination of Alexander Chastain, indicated he may have yet another connection to the senator. Ted thought to himself, *if what Tony said is true, does it mean he took it upon himself to punish Chastain? Am I representing a vigilante?* Ted knew if that were the case, the likelihood of a successful insanity defense was highly improbable.

His next thoughts turned to his older sister Elizabeth and what happened to her so many years ago...and how that event had destroyed his family. Lizzie never recovered from it; it took away her future...and it hastened the death of his father who was emasculated by his inability to redress the wrong. In many different ways, it meant a loss to Ted of his loving older sister and it taught Ted how to hate more deeply than he ever thought he could...or ever wanted to. Even this many years removed, he still harbored hope someone would do the bastard in. He looked back at the time and wished, despite his age, he would have exacted some retribution to avenge his sister. Would have...should have.

When his thoughts returned to Tony, he wondered if this Ranger had the balls he himself lacked. Did Tony even the score for Carrie Burk? Is that what this is all about? Could it possibly be true Carrie's violation was enough to push Icovatti over the edge, spur him to do more than just protest? Reagan's attempted assassin acted only out of his irrational infatuation with a movie star he had never met. Is this where Icovatti's mind also dwelled? The only connection between Carrie Burk and Tony Icovatti was they were residents of the same facility; they weren't related, they never knew each other before...or maybe they did? Maybe, in the mind of a vigilante, there didn't need to be more of a connection.

Ted made a mental note to ask Mike, his paralegal, to check out the Burk gun shop as soon as possible.

Book II: The Coming Trial

The Sunday Morning Roundtable

Carson Nelson: Good Sunday morning everyone and welcome to another edition of The Roundtable. Today marks five-and-a-half months since the assassination of Senator Alexander Chastain, and this morning we are devoting the entire telecast to a discussion of what we have learned so far and what we can expect in the trial which begins in two weeks. With us this morning, we are fortunate to have Ms. Terri Breckenridge, the Washington Bureau Chief for *The New York Times* and Michael Muelheim, one of New York's finest criminal defense lawyers. Good morning to you both.

Breckenridge: Good morning, Carson.

Muelheim: Good morning. Good to be here.

Nelson: Michael, let's start with you. One of the first questions our viewers may have is why is this case in the local county court in Cleveland instead of in Federal District Court? I was under the impression this is a federal offense.

Muelheim: Carson, that's a good question. It is a federal offense, but it is also a violation of the laws of the State of Ohio. The Code of

Federal Regulations tells us in a case such as this there is concurrent jurisdiction. That means the prosecution of the accused can be pursued in either Federal District Court or in the local county court. The CFR also tells us the Federal District Attorney really controls the venue. If the District Attorney's Office wants it in Federal Court, it must be pursued there. For reasons known only to them, they elected to stay out of Federal Court and let it proceed in Cuyahoga County.

Nelson: Do you believe there is a political reason behind that decision? Chastain was a Democrat whereas the District Attorney was appointed by President Bush.

Muelheim: I don't believe so but I don't know for sure. Certainly one would think the District Attorney would like this conviction on his resume. As it turns out, the State's case will be pursued by the Prosecutor for Cuyahoga County, J. Michael Gerrity.

Nelson: Terri, I understand Gerrity is a powerful figure in the Democratic Party in Northern Ohio.

Breckenridge: Yes, he is the Chairman of the Democratic Party for Cuyahoga County and he has held that position for the last twelve years or so; nothing really happens within the party in Northern Ohio without his approval. Rumor has it he is interested in higher office.

Nelson: Congress?

Breckenridge: Perhaps, or maybe the governor's office.

Nelson: So...the State will be represented by Gerrity. Now this Ted Chase fellow…what do we know about him?

Breckenridge: Not much, Carson. Local fellow from Icovatti's hometown, Crawford. Not much of a resume. Member of a very small firm. He has done some criminal defense work, but certainly nothing notable. He's never been on a stage of this magnitude, that's for sure. But…to be fair…not many attorneys have.

Nelson: Michael, what do you think about a local guy like Chase representing a man accused of killing a presidential candidate in a trial which will be watched by the entire planet?

Muelheim: Carson, I only hope he recognized what he "signed up" for when he decided to handle the case. Some attorneys, especially those who do criminal defense work, at times let their egos get in the way of their decision making.

Nelson: So you think this fellow may be in over his head. Death is an option here, isn't it?

Muelheim: Yes, it is. As far as Chase being in over his head, no, can't say that for sure. He may do just fine. But…he is pursuing an insanity verdict in a case where there appears, at least to me, to be quite a bit of planning and forethought.

Nelson: Yes, let's discuss the insanity thing. First of all, how does one continue to pursue a not guilty-by-reason-of-insanity verdict after his client has already been found by the court to be fit to stand trial?

Muelheim: Nelson, the standards are different and so is the decision-maker. In Cuyahoga County, cases are assigned to judges on a random basis. As we all know, Judge Martin Delsander was the draw, and it was Judge Delsander who had to determine Icovatti's fitness for trial. After the competency hearing, he determined Icovatti understood the charges against him and could aid his attorney in his defense. It is not a high standard. A finding of innocence or guilt, however, is left to the jury. In this case, the jury must determine beyond a reasonable doubt Icovatti did the deed, and at the time he did it, he fully understood right from wrong. I would offer John Hinkley, Jr. as an example.

Nelson: The young man who shot President Reagan.

Muelheim: That's right. He, too, was found competent to stand trial, but at trial, his attorneys successfully proved he only did what he did because he was trying to impress actress Jodie Foster. He was insanely obsessed with her to a degree he could not tell right from wrong. He was found not guilty by reason of insanity. Though found not guilty, he has been institutionalized ever since.

Nelson: That was my next question. The accused could be found not guilty by reason of insanity yet the court retains jurisdiction over him. How is that?

Muelheim: Carson, that's what most people don't understand. A finding of not guilty by reason of insanity doesn't give the accused a "walk." He's committed to an appropriate mental health institution by the court. The court then maintains jurisdiction over the defendant for the same amount of time the defendant could have served in prison had he been found guilty of the crime. In Hinkley's case, and in this case too, that would be the remainder of his life because a life sentence without parole is "in play" here.

Nelson: You mentioned "planning and forethought." I assume you believe evidence of planning cuts against an insanity verdict.

Muelheim: Yes. It is much harder to prove an individual doesn't know right from wrong if he planned out the act over a long period of time, took covert action to bring it about, and then tried to cover it up. All that is an indication he was fully aware what he was doing was wrong.

Nelson: I see. Terri, you wrote an article earlier about the experts who testified at the competency hearing.

Breckenridge: Yes, Doctors Berringer and Hickman.

Nelson: Do you think they will be called to testify at the trial?

Breckenridge: Yes, it is very likely. Berringer has been treating Icovatti since his return from Iraq.

Nelson: And Hickman?

Breckenridge: Well...we've seen him before on the national stage. You may recall *State vs. Swanson*, the case of the California heiress accused of murdering her parents. More of a "hired gun," if you will. Johns Hopkins. Very smooth in court.

Nelson: Advantage Hickman?

Breckenridge: Probably.

Nelson: Let's talk jury. Icovatti was seriously wounded in service to his country in Iraq. That should resonate with the jury, wouldn't you think?

Breckenridge: Certainly.

Nelson: And where will the jurors come from?

Breckenridge: Cuyahoga County...mostly liberal, blue collar, largely Democratic, heavily minority.

Nelson: That brings me back to the question I asked earlier about why the prosecution was not pursued on the federal level. Liberal, blue-collar Democrats would certainly mourn the death of Alexander Chastain; they were his power base. Michael?

Muelheim: No doubt. But liberals considering a criminal case are sometimes more likely to give the defendant a pass...regardless of the evidence. Jury nullification is the new reality.

Nelson: Jury nullification...you mean like OJ.

Muelheim: That's right, Carson. There was a mountain of evidence pointing to Simpson's guilt but the jury gave him a pass...and there was no question of mental competence in that case.

Nelson: So if it's close, an insanity verdict may present itself as an acceptable compromise to a Cuyahoga County jury?

Muelheim: Could be.

Nelson: Why was there also a straight "not guilty" plea entered by the defense?

Muelheim: Standard defense move. Chase wants to maintain all his options. You never know how the evidence is going to come in… or what the judge may keep out.

Nelson: Terri, where is Tony Icovatti?

Breckenridge: Carson, we don't know for sure. At Icovatti's arraignment, Chase convinced Judge Delsander he should be kept at an undisclosed location until trial...for security purposes. Rumor has it there had been threats.

Nelson: So no one knows.

Breckenridge: Let's put it this way. Neither the press nor the general public knows.

Nelson: Okay...let's talk evidence. A high-powered rifle stolen from a gun shop in Icovatti's hometown allegedly has Icovatti's fingerprints on it. An FBI file documenting Icovatti had been stalking Chastain for a number of months. Icovatti in Cleveland for the rally but allegedly "missing" at the time the fatal shot was fired…

At this, Dorie Chase picked up the remote and clicked off the set. Ted continued to stare blankly at the darkened screen. The last twenty-two weeks of his life had been a living hell for him, his family, and his firm and...it was about to get worse. He closed his eyes contemplating the trial which was about to begin, and he wished "the cup would pass," but he knew it would not. It was true Ted had entered two pleas on behalf of his client but, even at this late date, with trial commencing in two weeks, he was uncertain how he was going to proceed. The "final push" would begin tomorrow.

The Offices of Rosenthal Chase

Ted took a sip of his hot black coffee from the mug which proclaimed he was the WORLD'S GREATEST DAD and then turned to Mac and Mike and said, "Okay, let's go over it all again."

Mike had the large conference table covered end to end with documents for the case of *The State of Ohio vs. Anthony Icovatti.* The FBI's file on Tony, the ballistics report, the Crawford Police report of the Burk Gun Shop break in, both Berringer's and Hickman's psychiatric examination reports, multiple gruesome television videos of the last minutes of Chastain' life, transcripts of the competency hearing before Judge Delsander (which Carson Nelson correctly reported Ted had lost—Tony was found competent to stand trial), and Tony's arrest record from Cuyahoga County were all there, along with a binder of Tony's St. Joseph's treatment records.

Mike asked, "Where do you want to start?"

Ted responded, "Let's look at the ballistics first."

Mike opened that file and withdrew the ballistic report prepared for the Federal Bureau of Investigation. He pulled out several pictures of the M24 and laid them on the table. "Okay…we have the M24, the murder weapon."

"Mike, you were at Burk's gun shop. Ever see an M24?"

"You know...I might have. When you walk in, there is a display counter right in the middle of the store. There was a rifle in a mount right on top. It's the first thing to catch your eye when you walk in. May have been a 24. It had a scope on it. Don't know for sure."

"Well what do we know about M24s?"

"It is the military and law enforcement version of the Remington 700. For a time, it was the standard issue United States Army sniper rifle. I did a little internet research on it. About fifteen thousand of them were produced beginning in 1988. Says here the M24 has the 'long action' bolt version of the Remington 700 because, originally, it was supposed to use thirty-ot-six ammunition. Turns out there was some issue there, so the operational requirement was changed to use something smaller called the NATO Ml 18 Match Grade cartridge. That was the size of the bullet that blew the back of Chastain's head off and...there was a perfect match to our weapon."

"The FBI lab matched the grooves on the bullet to the M24's barrel."

"Yep. They discharge another round from the M24 into a water tank, retrieve it and place it under a microscope right next to the fatal bullet to compare the grooves. Here's the picture," handing it to Ted.

Mac, too, looked at the picture of the two bullets and said, "Perfect match."

"Appears that way," responded Ted. "Well, what do you think? Still nothing of any use to us here."

Both Mac and Mike nodded.

"Okay, let's look at the print evidence."

Mike retrieved another set of pictures. "Here are the prints lifted from the murder weapon and here are Tony's."

The State had Tony's prints assembled on a transparency which could be laid over the top of the prints lifted from the weapon. Mike did so.

"Another perfect match," said Mac.

Ted just shook his head. "How many other prints did you say were lifted from the rifle?"

"None."

Mac shot a look at Ted who smiled back but said nothing.

"Anything else found on the rifle?"

Mike returned to the ballistics report and flipped through the pages. "You know, I missed this before. There were traces of alcohol."

"Alcohol? Interesting. What do you make of that, Mac?"

"Not sure."

"Okay. We're talking a rifle here, not handguns, so I assume we have no residue issues."

Mike responded, "There was not enough residue to even conduct a test."

Ted turned to his co-counsel, "Mac, what do you think we have here? No residue evidence in the case but only the one set of fingerprints on the murder weapon and they're our guy's..."

Mac responded, "Good and bad."

"Yeah. Mike, do we know how much time elapsed after Chastain was shot and before the Feds got to Tony?"

"No. I looked into that last time we discussed. it. All we know is Neary told the FBI Tony was not with them when the shot was fired."

"And we don't know exactly where Tony was?"

"That's right. Tony was no help to us on that."

Ted stroked his chin, "Tony has been no help to us on much of anything. Berringer says he is actually regressing."

Mac spoke up, "Ted, should we be talking with Berringer again? Perhaps consider filing a motion for reconsideration of the Court's ruling on competency? After all, it has been almost three months since the hearing and, as you say, it appears our client is getting worse and has been of no help to us."

"We certainly should consider it. Problem here is it seems Tony goes 'in and out.' Sometimes he is fine, lucid; other times I can't tell what planet he is on. They really are doing everything for him now at St. Joseph's. In fact, I was thinking of asking Berringer to leave Tony completely on his own for about a week before trial."

Mike said, "I'm sorry?"

Mac spoke up, "Ted wants the jury to see what Tony is like on his own...without any help from anyone taking care of him. You could have a problem there, Ted."'

"Yeah, I know. I know. But is it really fair? The Court may have some issues with us if we don't present a clean-cut defendant in a new suit but...really...that's not the way he is now. At least not without a ton of help. What's the worst that could happen?"

"Delsander could take us to task in front of the jury...which will make it look like we're pulling a fast one. We need to be very careful here."

"Yeah, you're probably right. I'll have to think about it some more. Mike, let's take another look at the gun shop break-in stuff."

"Really don't have much there either. The owner reported the break-in three days before the Cleveland rally. Here are the pictures the Crawford Police Department took. Appears the rear door to the shop was pried open with a crowbar or something similar."

"Owner's name is Bobby Burk?"

"Right."

"Wife was the one reported in the papers?"

"Carrie."

Ted looked at the pictures of the rear door of the shop. "And nothing else was taken, is that right?"

"Nothing else, just the M24."

At this, Mac shot another look at Ted then asked Mike, "A shop full of weapons and ammunition which have immense value on the street and nothing but one rifle was taken? Any cameras in the store?"

"No."

"Any other evidence...prints?"

"No."

"And the police have no other leads at all?"

"If they do, they're not pursuing them."

Ted said, "There's another connection Tony has with the gun shop and I'm quite certain we're the only ones who know about it. Not sure it helps us though."

Mac responded, "And what would that be?"

"Tony has the room right next to Carrie Burk's at St. Joseph's. Last time I met with him and Berringer, Tony told us Carrie Burk was raped."

"Yeah...so?"

"On Chastain's campaign bus."

"What?"

"Tony swears Carrie Burk was raped on Chastain's bus because she told him. Berringer knew nothing about it."

Mac was speechless. He needed time to think. "Next thing you're going to tell us is it was Chastain who did the deed."

"Him and others."

"Oh my God. Ted, do we know this for a fact?"

"All we know for certain is our client, who we may try to prove is insane, told us that."

"Jesus Christ..."

"Right."

Mike spoke up, "What does that mean for us...for our case?"

Ted responded, "Right now, I'm uncertain. Mac, any thoughts?"

"I think if Gerrity gets a hold of that information, the 'spin' will be it was like throwing gas on a fire. Look at it this way. Tony is at St. Joseph's, already has major issues with Chastain, and then finds out Chastain and his cronies raped the Burk woman. Now, that's all he needs...so he makes a decision to take him out. It transforms him into a Don Quixote on an honorable quest rather than a disgruntled, forever damaged veteran pissed at the world. And Ted, you make a good point. Let's say somehow the information is helpful to us and we want to use it. How do we come across if we ask the jury to buy into Tony's testimony when our goal may be for them to find him insane?"

Ted responded, "But consider this. What if it is false; only conjured up in Tony's mind? Isn't that proof of insanity? Tony takes out Chastain to avenge a rape that never really occurred. He acted only because of his delusion."

"Well, you've got a really good point there. That would fit. But unless we know for sure what happened to Carrie Burk, we can't 'go there.' Much too dangerous."

Ted knew Mac was right. He would continue to struggle with Tony's revelation about Carrie Burk and what it could mean to the presentation of his client's case. Long ago, he recognized juries do not appreciate "pleading in the alternative" (our guy didn't do it but if he did do it, he was insane when he did it). But even this near the trial, Ted seemingly could not walk away from either theory of defense; there will still too many unanswered questions. Would he be forced to proceed this way at trial? He hated where he was; uncertainty in the defense of any criminal charge is suicide.

Ted nodded. "Mike, let's review the video again. The best one is from CNN."

Mike took that disc out of its sheath and placed it in his laptop. Before too long, the image of a good-looking, glad-handing Alexander Chastain in the final moments of his life filled the screen. Even now, after they had viewed it so many times, the recording was difficult to watch. During the twelve-minute run time, Ted asked Mike several times to stop the replay and back it up. He would stare at it for some time and then motion Mike to resume the play. There didn't appear to be anything of help to them.

"Okay. I've seen enough."

"Ted, I know you are totally familiar with Hickman's and Berringer's reports from the competency hearing, but do you want to go over them again?" asked Mike.

"Yes, but not right now. I will do that at home on my own time. Please put both reports and the Berringer's treatment records on Tony in my large briefcase."

Mac spoke up, "Well what do you think, Ted? Is it just going to end up being a battle of the experts? Hickman is going to say Tony studied Chastain for months...even to the point of collecting magazine articles, successfully broke into a gun shop in his hometown without leaving a clue, went to Cleveland on his own, executed a perfect shot, one perhaps only a Ranger marksman could pull off, and planned the whole thing so he could be far enough away to be undetected. Perfect calculation and design. Certainly conduct of a man who knew the consequences of his actions. Tony only made one mistake...leaving his prints on the weapon."

Ted saw an opportunity to "take a shot" at Mac, "A law professor once taught me to look at the big picture and then take it apart piece by piece. We've certainly got the big picture...and it doesn't look good. But we need to break it apart. We've got two more weeks. I'm going to visit the gun shop when we're done here. Need to see it for myself. Mike, what time is our final pretrial with Delsander tomorrow?"

"One thirty."

"Okay. I'm going over to Burk's and then I'm going to review the reports and treatment records again tonight at home. Mac and I will have to leave here about noon to get to Cleveland. Mac, I'll pick you up at your place. That okay?"

"Works for me."

"Okay, I'll see you tomorrow. And both of you give some thought to why there was only one set of prints on the weapon and think about the Carrie Burk thing...and we can talk some more."

Burk's Gun Shop

It was as Mike reported. The shop was not large but very neat and well organized, reflecting the character of its owner. Wild game on the walls near the ceiling included some nice bucks and several ram. Much like a jewelry shop, glass display cases framed the store leaving just enough room between them and the walls for the proprietor to walk behind. There was enough floor space in the middle for a separate, stand-alone case which had a singular gun mount on its top where one rifle was prominently displayed. The wall space higher than the display cases and below the mounted dead animals was filled with every manner of handgun including some reproductions. Directly opposite the entrance against the back wall and behind the main display case was a workbench with a high back. It was covered with tools and had a vice and some other electric fixtures Ted did not recognize but assumed were necessary to work on firearms. On the bench were parts of a rifle, workshop rags, cans of fluids including lubricants and cleaning solutions and a box of green latex surgical gloves. The cash register was on a separate table tucked in the corner, framed by NRA posters on the walls behind it and to the side. There was a round surveillance mirror mounted diagonally from the cash register, up near the ceiling, which captured both the register and the front door. A small bell was mounted on the doorframe and sounded when the door opened. The entry to the rear storage room was in between the end of the workbench and the register in the corner. Bobby Lee Burk came out from the back room when he heard the bell. Ted could tell from the rifle dismantled on the workbench and from the apron and latex gloves he was wearing that Bobby Lee was in the middle of a project. Right on Ted's heels, the bell sounded again and a young, rather gruff looking, fully bearded, individual entered. His dirty blonde ponytail hung from the back of his red, white and blue bandana and partially covered the barbed wire tattoo which encircled his neck. He wore a camouflage vest, ragged blue jeans, and ornate cowboy boots. From the right side of his belt hung a hunting knife in a leather sheath and from the left, a rather large silver chain that was connected to a big black billfold bulging out of his back pocket. He made a beeline to the center display case.

Bobby Lee was no dummy; he knew how to sell. Early on he recognized the first thing to attract the attention of his customers as they entered the shop was the center case and whatever he could display on its top. What he always did was place a top-of-the-line firearm in the mount, one that carried a healthy markup. True to form, "bandana man" picked up the rifle, examined it for a bit, placed the stock against his right shoulder and then closed his left eye as if aiming at a trophy buck, or perhaps, something else. Burk watched with a smile on his face as he peeled off the latex gloves. "Never fails," he muttered to himself. Ted was silently watching both men and he chuckled just a bit when he overheard Bobby Lee.

It was instantly apparent Bobby Lee was going to be occupied for a bit so Ted said, "I need to make a phone call. I'll be right back." Burk nodded and turned to his customer. He hated that Ted was leaving, but he was looking at a profit of over two hundred dollars if he closed a sale with "ponytail boy." What Ted hated was that any guy looking like Burk's new customer could waltz into a gun shop and exercise his "Second Amendment right" to purchase a weapon which could put a bullet in a human being from a thousand yards away. "Political correctness" had never been Ted's strong suit, and, let's face it, the NRA had effectively promoted their astonishing discovery: "Guns don't kill people, people kill people." Guns just make it a helluva lot easier.

The Chase Home

It was not unusual for Ted to bring work home, but his cardinal rule was he did not touch a file until the kids were in bed for the night. What most non-lawyers don't appreciate about the practice of law is the amount of behind-the-scene time a lawyer must put in to be ready for the following day's events—especially true for the relatively small percentage of lawyers who do trial work.

The overall public perception of a lawyer is someone on his feet, making arguments in a courtroom, but the truth of the matter is the vast majority of lawyers never set foot in one; a litigation practice demands way too much homework.

Ted preferred to re-review the psychiatric evaluations of the experts while in the comfort of his recliner...with two fingers of Glenlivet. Increased use of experts in litigation was the trend and that sometimes invited abuse. Any lawyer, if he looked hard enough, could find an expert in any field who, for a price, would say what the lawyer needed him to say. The "failure" in the system clearly rested at the feet of the lawyers who used unscrupulous experts whose opinions were "for sale." Anyone who had engaged in asbestos litigation was certainly familiar with this concept. Ted had read quite a bit about Dr. Hickman and had seen him several times on the national news. He realized Hickman was the key: The jury "buys into" his opinion on sanity and Tony is "toast." They reject it and there is a chance. Ted had to find a way to "attack" the doctor's opinion without attacking the man.

From past experience, Ted also realized when it came to expert testimony, for some odd reason, juries sometimes considered what Ted called "the travel factor"—the farther the distance the expert travelled to appear in court, the more credibility he or she garnered with the jury, especially if he came from either coast. It was total bunk, but sadly could not be ignored and had to be dealt with. It was certainly present here and was compounded by Hickman's association with Johns Hopkins, perhaps the finest medical school in the nation. Ted was making notes on his legal pad as he slowly perused Hickman's evaluation. It was readily apparent to Ted that Hickman had the luxury of examining Tony on one of Tony's "good" days.

The interview included a discussion of Tony's family and then more about Salvatore Colonna, whose horrific death brought Tony to his present state. But there was no indication Hickman had any clue about Tony's connection (real or imagined) with the wife of the gun shop owner.

Hickman interpreted the raw data from Berringer's psychiatric testing of Tony rather than perform any testing of his own. Ted made several notes which would later become the outline for his cross examination of the State's "celebrity" psychiatrist. He also made himself a note to confer with Dr. Berringer to review Hickman's report with him. Ted hoped Berringer might be able to provide additional insight Ted could use in his cross examination.

On the issue of Tony's sanity, the Bureau's fingerprint evidence was also perplexing because, to Ted, it didn't seem to "fit." The State maintained Tony was sane when he planned Chastain's murder, but wouldn't a sane man planning a murder take steps to prevent the weapon from being "traced" back to him? Leaving fingerprints on it and then leaving it behind certainly didn't make much sense.

The Justice Center, Cleveland, Ohio

The two towers of the Justice Center, only two blocks from the warehouse district where Chastain's life ended, housed the Clerk's office, the Sheriff's Department, the Cleveland Police Department, the County Jail and the Common Pleas courtrooms. There were four rooms (A through D) on each floor of the court tower and Delsander's was Courtroom 27B. This was the defense team's second visit to the Justice Center. At Tony's arraignment, Ted had persuaded the presiding judge to provide them with two free parking passes so they could park beneath the building. Ted had presented the request to the judge based upon his concern for security. An ancillary benefit from this parking arrangement was it allowed the defense team to avoid the outside of the building with its swirling debris, cigarette butts ground into the pavement, sick smelling hot dog carts, and county employees with fags hanging from their lips loitering on picnic tables enveloped by plumes of cancer-causing smoke. Not far from the main entrance stood a rather large and, Ted was told, expensive sculpture, which looked to Ted like twisted black sewer pipes welded into a shape somewhat resembling a discarded paper clip. Unfortunately, upon entering the building, it was necessary for the defense team to switch elevators at the ground floor atrium (which leaked) and there they became "fair game" for the press and TV reporters who routinely accosted them. The court tower was not designed with enough elevators to service it so, once inside, you had to queue up and wait to go up to your courtroom. Since cutting-in-line was raised to an art form at this location, getting inside an elevator took much longer than it should have. The Icovattis had shared with Ted Cleveland's Justice Center reminded them of a huge public toilet and they were "spot-on." Ted compared it to its impeccably clean and well-maintained counterpart in Franklin County (Columbus) and believed the residents and elected officials of Cuyahoga County would be totally ashamed and embarrassed...had they known any better.

While waiting for the next elevator, Mac and Ted were surrounded by the media making it even harder for them to move forward in line. After being pelted with question after question they were not about to answer and having the shoulder-mounted television cameras thrust in their faces one too many times, Ted had finally had enough. In as calm a voice as he could summon, he said, "Listen folks, last time we were here, we told you we could not answer any of your questions. What I did share with you last time is unchanged; Corporal Icovatti is innocent of this crime and that is pretty much all you need to know. I understand you all have jobs to do but so do we. Once the trial is underway in a couple weeks, I am certain you will have plenty to report. Thank you very much." (Ted had to choose his words carefully; no doubt prospective jurors would hear them this evening when they turned on their sets and listened to the news.) The questions, however, never stopped until the elevator doors closed and they were on the way to Delsander's room which, as a result of his pretrial order, was "off limits" to the media...at least for now.

The courtrooms themselves were also something to behold; the designer must have been high on one substance or another or perhaps had double vision. The walls were covered by one-inch wood strips about two inches apart running floor to ceiling. Those having to look at the walls for any length of time (a juror sitting on a big case, for instance) routinely experienced dizziness and sometimes even motion sickness. Recognizing this, at least one judge covered up the walls of his courtroom by hanging very large, colorful, polyester flags.

J. Michael Gerrity and very young Assistant Prosecutor Kurland were waiting for Ted and Mac in the bailiff's hallway outside Delsander's chambers. Gerrity's lead prosecutor in the Major Crimes Division was a seasoned litigator by the name of Neal Craddock and Ted thought it interesting Craddock was not assigned the case. Gerrity's entire office was also buzzing after the selection of greenhorn Kurland as Gerrity's second chair. The other young lawyers in Kurland's hire-in "class" were green with envy and wondered how much sucking-up Kurland had engaged in. Craddock wasn't envious; he was pissed, but he understood. He figured Gerrity saw the case as a "lock" and was not about to share the credit for a conviction with anyone and, of course, Craddock was right.

Ted steadfastly believed opponents in litigation must always exhibit a mutual respect and decorum, but Gerrity greeted Mac and Ted as though they were longstanding members of his Saturday morning foursome instead of two lawyers he had never dealt with and had met just once before. It seemed a bit contrived, "Ted and Mac how the heck have you been?"

At this stage in the proceedings, Ted did not desire that degree of false familiarity with Gerrity. "We are fine, thanks for asking." He deliberately did not inquire about their well-being but instead looked at the bailiff, "Is the judge ready for us?"

Ted could see Gerrity was somewhat put off, thinking it a bit of a snub in front of his young assistant, but for now, that didn't bother Ted.

Rising, the bailiff said, "Yes, give me a second to tell him everyone is here; I'm sure he'll want you to come right back."

Ignoring Gerrity, Ted turned to look out the large windows in the bailiff area which offered a panoramic view of the Cleveland Browns football stadium, the break wall, and Lake Erie beyond. To the east, one could see Lakefront Airport, and to the west, the Port of Cleveland docks with the ore boats being unloaded. Interstate 90 was also visible closer to the building running parallel to a major rail artery which connected the Great Lakes region to the east coast. You could see moving trains, planes, and automobiles as well as the lake freighters...all from one vantage point. Any young boy would have been enthralled; looking down from that height, it all appeared to be a huge electric toy set being operated from unseen transformers.

Judge Delsander followed his bailiff back to the door of his chambers and invited them in. "Welcome, welcome. Mike...Ted. Welcome back to Cleveland Professor McIlvaine." (Like most jurists in Cleveland, Delsander was very familiar with Ted's co-counsel.) He only nodded at Kurland because he couldn't remember his name.

The judge walked to the head of his large conference table which sat in front of his desk, "Everyone, please sit. Make yourselves comfortable." Looking at Ted and Mac, "How was the trip in?"

Ted responded, "It was fine, Judge. No problems."

"Well...good, good. How is everyone holding up?"

Smiles all around. Gerrity spoke up, "About as well as can be expected. Be glad when this is all over."

"Well, we start in two weeks. So how's it going so far? I haven't heard from anybody so I assume there are no discovery issues. Mike?"

Looking at Ted, Gerrity responded, "No, don't think so. We have provided everything the defense has requested."

"Ted?"

"No issues there, Judge."

"Well, good then."

Delsander wanted to discuss the testimony and he had his pen poised to take notes. "Mike, what are we looking at here?"

"Well, Your Honor, my goal is to keep things simple; it seems the entire world witnessed the deed. If counsel and I can agree, I would like to start out with one of the network videos. It certainly would be the best evidence of what occurred. "

"You want to show a video to the jury of the fatal shot?"

"Yes."

"Ted? What do you think?"

"Not sure it's necessary but I won't object as long as there is an agreement on which video."

Delsander said, "Good. Mike, when you and Ted settle on one, make sure my staff attorney gets a copy."

Gerrity nodded and resumed, "We have the Cuyahoga Coroner on the cause of death and the FBI agent on the prints and ballistics. We also intend to call Tim Neary to document Icovatti's whereabouts on the day of the murder and months before..."

"Neary?"

"He is the veteran Icovatti hooked up with. He was here in Cleveland when Chastain was shot."

"Okay."

"We also have the gun shop owner from Icovatti's hometown, who had the rifle stolen from his shop."

Holding his pen up, Delsander asked, "And what is his name?"

"Burk, Bobby Lee Burk."

Writing, "Okay."

"And, as you know, our expert on sanity is Dr. Hickman."

"Yes."

"Believe it or not, Your Honor, that's about it."

"Really? I guess you're serious about keeping it simple."

Looking at Ted rather than Delsander, Gerrity responded, "Your Honor, we believe the State's evidence is pretty straightforward."

Turning to Ted, "And you, Ted?"

Five months ago, Ted had entered two pleas on behalf of his client: not guilty and not guilty by reason of insanity. In any layman's mind, these were inconsistent. One defense is "our guy did not do this thing" while the other is "yes, he did the act but only because he lacked the mental ability to know right from wrong." Pleading in the alternative. In the months leading up to this very moment, Ted had been considering and reconsidering the evidence against his client and weighing his options. He had to settle upon a strategy and defense presenting the best chance of saving Tony's life. The "talking heads" were right; a jury finding of not guilty by reason of insanity was far less a desirable outcome than a straight not guilty; the Court would retain jurisdiction over Tony, probably for the remainder of his life. While the penitentiary would not be an option, confinement to a facility for the insane certainly would and Ted's thoughts turned to John Hinkley. Given the State's case against Tony, the NGRI route was the safest course, but Ted still had questions about the State's evidence; to Ted, it just didn't seem to add up. He was now required to share his witness list with the Court but even at this date so close to the trial, he wasn't about to forfeit either defense available to him. It appeared to Ted he may, indeed, need to present two theories to the jury.

"Our expert is the treating psychiatrist, Dr. Michael Berringer. We also intend to call six lay witnesses: Mr. and Mrs. Icovatti and their oldest son, Mr. and Mrs. Colonna, and an Army Ranger by the name of Stuyvesant Shanks."

"Colonna?"

"Their son, Salvatore Colonna, was Icovatti's best friend."

"This is the boy who was killed in Iraq?"

"Yes, Your Honor."

"And I assume this Shanks person was also in Iraq?"

"Yes. Icovatti's commanding officer. We, too, have Tim Neary on our witness list, but we can question him when the State calls him."

"Any witnesses addressing the ballistics or the prints?"

Ted intended to attack the State on the prints, but his strategy did not include calling his own witness on the issue. "No, Your Honor."

There was no discussion about whether or not Icovatti would take the stand. Delsander, as well as everyone else in the room, knew Ted was not about to make any commitment at this time and it was a waste of breath to even pose the question.

Delsander said, "I want to discuss media and security and then I want to go over jury selection with you. I understand all the major networks will share the feeds from the three cameras which will be temporarily installed in my courtroom. I have reviewed their plans and have determined for myself they are unobtrusive and won't interfere in our proceedings. My understanding is one camera is aimed at the bench and witness box, one takes in both counsel tables, and the third captures the public seating area in the rear of the room. My bailiff has the schematic. Each of you needs to review that and if you have any issues, bring those to the court's attention beforehand.

"There will be no inside-the-room coverage until after the jury is selected. During the proceedings, the jury will be shielded from the cameras one hundred percent of the time.

"Special arrangements have been made with my next-door neighbor here, Judge Donna Ratliff. She purposely scheduled a vacation to coincide with our trial so we could use her courtroom as a temporary media center. The reporters will all be set up in there. When we're done here, my bailiff will take you next door and show you how all that will work.

"You already have my pretrial order. It will be provided to the media; it does not permit them to engage the lawyers in any manner during the trial. No questions or interviews of any sort. I have scheduled a conference in two days; they will be told the news organization they represent will be banned if there is an attempt to circumvent my order in any way. You are all welcome to attend that conference or send a representative if you wish.

"Unfortunately, the other two rooms across the hall from us here have to continue to conduct business so that means there will be a lot of people coming and going from the floor. Additional security will be set up at the elevators including two additional metal scanners. There will also be a full contingent of deputies on the floor with at least two posted at the doors to our room. I understand anyone who gets a seat in the courtroom will be given some sort of badge they must wear. You may know there is a special bank of elevators and a separate hallway for the judges behind these chambers and I understand those areas will have additional security as well.

"With the exception of counsel, no mobile devices of any sort will be allowed in the courtroom; my order states they will be confiscated and a One Hundred-Dollar fine levied before they can be returned. Any questions so far?"

Ted spoke up. "Microphones?"

"Oh yes, thank you. I forgot. My understanding is the sound feed will not pick up any conversation you have at table and nothing from the jury box but everything else can be heard. I am told I will have an on/off switch at my bench which allows me to control all the audio in the entire courtroom. As long as I remember that, sidebar conferences should be no problem. Please remind me if you see I have forgotten...which is very likely to happen. Any other questions?"

Silence.

"The jury questionnaires continue to come in. I have asked our clerk to start with one hundred and fifty. I have also asked him to set up a secure site on his webpage. When you leave here today, you'll need to stop at his office on the first floor to receive your own secure password. I understand you will have on-line access as early as this afternoon to the questionnaires which have already been posted. All the questionnaires should be on the site by this Friday at the latest. I prefer you do not print hard copy, but if you must, dissemination is forbidden; it's part of my pretrial order.

"My preferred method of jury selection is the struck method. I assume you are all familiar with that. We will start by bringing in the first fifty potential jurors. I will conduct the preliminary questioning of all fifty and then turn it over to Mike. Ted goes last. I ask you pay close attention and not address any issues with them I have already covered or which are covered by our questionnaire. I am somewhat liberal when it comes to what you may ask but I want no discussion of what the law says or does not say and I do not what you exacting any promises from them based upon what you think the evidence may or may not show. After Ted is done, we will go into chambers with the court reporter. We will start with challenges for cause which I will rule upon. We will then move to the peremptories. Mike goes first, then Ted...back and forth. If we can reach an agreement on fourteen, we're done. If we're short of fourteen, we'll bring up the next twenty-five and start the process all over again with them until we reach fourteen.

I do allow the jurors to take notes but I do not allow them to ask questions. I don't believe in that. (That part was music to the ears of all the lawyers in the room.) Their notepads will be collected at the end of each day and kept here in my chambers. No one will be permitted to see them during the trial. For purposes of appeal, they will be kept as part of the record."

Ted spoke up, "Your Honor, how do you select the two alternates?"

"Good question. Once we settle upon the fourteen who will hear the case, we won't designate which two are the alternates until after both of you have rested. I want each juror to pay very close attention to the presentation of your evidence and also my jury instructions to them; I don't want anyone 'slacking' because he or she had been designated an alternate right at the start of the trial."

The judge leaned back in his chair and reached over to his desk and brought forth a jar containing fourteen small slips of yellow construction paper, numbered one through fourteen, which were folded in half. He set the jar on his conference table in front of the lawyers. "We will randomly draw two numbers from this jar and the corresponding jurors will become our alternates. Any questions?"

Gerrity stated, "I assume sequestration."

"Yes. The clerk has made arrangements for them at the Marriott right across the street from us here; half a floor with round-the-clock security. They will take breakfast and dinner in the hotel and will have no access to live media of any sort. I understand arrangements are being made to have available an extensive library of existing programming, movies…that sort of thing. I had hoped to get underway Tuesday after this, but due to all these arrangements being made, I'm told a week from Thursday is a more realistic goal. Given the amount of time it will take to seat the jury, I see no problem starting on a Thursday."

The Return Trip

Once in the car, Ted turned to Mac, "Well it appears Delsander has everything well in hand."

"That's for sure and thank goodness. Lance Ito, he definitely ain't."

"I was relieved he favors the struck method of jury selection as opposed to the old-fashioned way. Nothing worse than standing up in front of a jury and excusing one of their members, with the rest wondering why you did it and perhaps holding it against you. I prefer it when the judge simply returns to the bench from chambers and announces who is on the panel and who is excused. No one is the wiser."

Mac said, "I agree. Also happy he does not let them ask questions. Allowing jurors to ask questions is unconstitutional, in my humble opinion. Encroaches upon the right to counsel."

"You never had a humble opinion your life." Ted chuckled. "But I agree. We'll have to get Mike working on the jury questionnaires as soon as we can. He'll need some help. I'm sure there will be reams of information out in cyberspace on each juror. He'll need to track that all down. Mac, you know of any third-years who may be able to help? They'll have to work out of our office though; can't risk it any other way."

"Don't think that will pose a problem. They'll become part of the defense team in the 'trial of the decade.' I'm pretty sure any law student looking for a job at the end of the year would like that on a resume. I'll call the Dean. Already have a good idea who one could be."

"Danny Longer?"

Mac just smiled. "So who do we want on this jury?"

"Well, I'm thinking veterans...and mothers...for starters. Probably those who lean toward the conservative side of things? Not sure. What do you think?"

"Not sure either, Ted. I really need to give that a lot of thought; lots of 'angles' to consider here. Really depends on which direction you're going with it. When are you getting back together with Berringer?"

"Tuesday."

"Good. So what do you think about Gerrity?"

"Well, I dunno. Seems more like he's a politician first and a lawyer second. But...he has the resources of the County, State, FBI, and probably the entire Justice Department at his disposal so we're definitely outgunned here. From the sound of things, he appears pretty cocksure he can get a straight 'guilty.' Seems to me he's 'skimpy' on the sanity though; appears to be putting all his eggs in Hickman's basket."

"Well, I'm sure he's looking at all the evidence he's got which establishes 'planning and design.' Our guy follows Chastain around for months, clips articles on him, steals a gun in his hometown—not just any gun—a sniper rifle allowing him to take the shot from far away, makes a special trip to Cleveland...Gerrity trots all that stuff out and then has Hickman tie it all together with his opinion that Icovatti knew exactly what he was doing and almost got away with it because he planned it so well. They buy into that and we're screwed."

'Yeah...for certain." Ted now felt even more dejected. The fate of a young man, a war hero no less...rested in Ted's hands. The enormity of it was almost too much for any one person to bear. At the conclusion of the trial, regardless of his success or failure, Ted would be returning to the comfort of his home and the love of his family. Where Tony Icovatti would be spending the remainder of his life, or how long a life he may have, would be decided by twelve people plucked from the voter rolls of Cuyahoga County.

For all his life, Ted firmly believed in America's system of jurisprudence; it was one of the reasons he chose the career he did. However, the fairest system of justice in the world, Ted believed, could never be fair enough to allow for the ultimate penalty. In order to permit that irreversible outcome, it really had to be much more than fair; it had to be perfect...and it was far from perfect. His thoughts shifted to his sister and his dead father. Not only was the bastard who defiled his sister not convicted...he was never even prosecuted; his family had too much money and too many connections. Lizzie received no justice and remained a victim her entire life...and it made a widow out of his mother.

When they got back to Crawford and arrived at Mac's condo, he opened the door to leave. Ted said, "Mac, Dorie and I are going to steal a weekend at the cottage...kinda' the calm before the storm. Inlaws will be watching the kids. I don't intend to work on anything law-related, but I'll have the cell so if anyone needs to, they can reach me. Hopefully, there will be no need."

"Ted, that's a good idea. Get some rest and recharge your batteries. I'll tell you what...if you want me to come up to keep Dorie occupied for you, no problem." Mac shut the door rather hard and laughed as he went up the walk to his front door.

Ted quickly lowered the passenger window and yelled, "You're an asshole!"

Mac flipped him the bird without turning around.

The Cottage

The in-laws' small cabin up at the lake was Ted and Dorie's retreat, a place where they could escape for a weekend to "recharge the batteries" just like Mac said. It had a rather small great room—kitchen, dining and living area with a wood burner in the hearth and only two bedrooms, one for Ted and Dorie and one for the in-laws, and a loft the kids absolutely loved. The place would always be very special to the two of them in a funny, but very intimate, way because when they were nineteen, this is where they snuck off to have sex for the first time. For his entire life, Ted would never forget how he felt while he drove Dorie to the cottage on that day.

The faded blue jeans, old golf shirt, and worn moccasins Ted kept in the closet of their bedroom and he couldn't wait to get there, put them on, and then build a fire in the cast iron wood burner. His favorite thing in the whole world was to sit with Dorie in his lap in the old leather chair with their feet on the ottoman and watch the flames' reflections dance on the cedar walls and the ceiling and listen to the crackle of the fire.

The cottage was less than an hour away and an added bonus was Hal's, their favorite restaurant, was right on the way. After stopping at Hal's for dinner, they arrived around ten. This night, they made no fire; they went right to sleep.

Because Dorie's parents took care of the financial end of having the cottage, Ted and Dorie were the self-appointed cleaners and caretakers.

The next morning at breakfast, Dorie announced their task for the morning was to clean the cottage's storm windows. She had everything ready except for the ladder which she asked Ted to retrieve from the cabin's shed.

Ted's job was to remove the window and bring it down to Dorie who was on the porch with all the cleaning supplies. She had the hose, which was hooked up to the outside well, a bucket full of sudsy water, several old bath towels, a roll of paper towel, and some spray cleaner. She handed Ted the only pair of rubber gloves she had. She wore tight blue jeans, her dad's tattered green flannel shirt and a red bandana which was wrapped around her forehead and tied in the back to hold back her hair. Ted thought she looked sexy in this getup and shared with her his fantasy about a cleaning lady but she laughed at him, told him to "get his mind out of the gutter" and get back to work. She hosed off the first small window Ted handed to her, washed it with the sudsy sponge, rinsed it with the hose and then dried it. She then took the spray cleaner to it and finished it off with paper towel. But when handing it back to Ted, she inadvertently smudged it in a few places. Ted took it up the ladder and replaced it in its frame.

But when she looked up at it, she yelled at Ted who was at the top of the ladder unscrewing the next storm. "Hey, Goober! Look at that!"

"What?"

"The window you just put back!"

"What about it?"

"You got your fingerprints all over it! It looks worse now than when you handed it to me, you Goober!" She was laughing.

Ted leaned over from the ladder to take a good look at the window. The morning sun highlighted the mess; fingerprint smudges covered two of its corners.

When he descended from the ladder with the window, he leaned it up against the porch's railing. Looking closer at the very small imprints on the window, he laughed and said, "You're the Goober. Those aren't my fingerprints. You're the one not wearing any gloves."

Dorie squinted and looked even closer. "Oops," was all she would say. Dorie sprayed the glass cleaner on the window again and wiped it with the paper towel.

Ted didn't move; it was like he was in a trance. He glanced at the rubber gloves he was wearing and then back to the window. His mind raced back to his visit to Burk's gun shop and "bandana man"...and he recalled his discussions with Mac and Mike about the Chastain weapon.

Dorie tried to hand the re-cleaned window to Ted but there was no reaction from him.

"Here, take this."

Ted didn't budge.

"Hello. Anybody home? Hello."

But nobody was home. Ted's mind was on his case.

Trial

Judge Martin Delsander arrived at the courthouse even earlier than normal. When he turned onto Lakeside Avenue, he was met with a sea of television trucks and trailers with their stanchions high in the air and their satellite dishes pointed toward the southwest. It looked to him more like an air defense installation rather than a few city blocks in downtown Cleveland. The Sheriff's Department had cordoned off a large area from Ontario Street to St. Clair to Lakeside, and it was necessary for the judge to pass through one of their temporary checkpoints to enter the driveway that led to the parking level under the Justice Center which was reserved for the Common Pleas Court judges.

Delsander knew he was about to leave his "mark" on history; the story of *The State of Ohio vs. Anthony Icovatti* could not be told without at least part of one "chapter" devoted to Martin Delsander, a mediocre student who graduated from law school by "the skin of his teeth" and was lucky to successfully navigate Ohio's bar exam on his second attempt. He wanted his law school classmates, including several who now directed the city's largest law firms, to seek him out for speaking engagements, black tie affairs, board memberships, and perhaps after retirement, "of counsel" status. This trial could well end up being his ticket to "easy street." Maybe even...a book. He had cleared his docket and been off the bench for the last three days so he could "rest up" and prepare.

At home for those three days, he had been pouring over his collection of tomes on evidence.

He arrived at his chambers behind Room 27B at 7:25 and turned the lights on and started brewing the coffee. Delsander wanted the additional hour to get himself mentally prepared. He had ordered Counsel to appear promptly at 8:30 with a goal of getting jury selection underway by 10:00.

Ted, Mac and Mike were in the hallway outside the bailiff's desk by 8:15 and Gerrity and Kurland arrived ten minutes later. They were immediately ushered into chambers where Delsander greeted them and offered coffee. After much small talk and comments about what was occurring outside the courtroom, Delsander got right down to business. "You have had my pretrial order for quite some time now and I expect you to follow it explicitly during the course of our proceedings. I have read your trial briefs and proposed jury instructions and it does not appear we have any issues regarding those. As we discussed at our last pretrial, the media has been informed the litigants are "off limits" to them for however long this may take. Please don't hesitate to inform me if any of you are approached in contravention of my order. As we all know, Senator Chastain held a very real chance to become our next President and his murder may be recorded in history as one that influenced the course of our nation. The prosecution's goal is to convict Mr. Icovatti of this crime whereas the defense's goal is to have him go home at the conclusion of the trial. My goal is to make sure the parties and all the lawyers are treated fairly and with respect and receive rulings from me consistent with the laws of our State. We must zealously guard Mr. Icovatti's rights here as well as the State's right to seek a conviction. The enormity of the case will not serve to compromise those rights in even the smallest regard; we are not going to let this become a media circus.

"We have the first fifty jurors in the courtroom with the first twelve already seated in the box. Since the questionnaires have been available to you since our last pretrial, nothing more will be provided to you this morning except the names of those the Court has already excused for hardship."

The judge's staff attorney was handing each side a list.

"As you can see, there is a notation in my own handwriting next to the name of each juror who has already been excused. Please scratch these names off your list. I believe there are a total of twelve, is that right, Ben?"

"Yes, Your Honor."

"Frankly, not bad out of a venire of one hundred and fifty. So we start with one hundred thirty-eight and, as I said, the first fifty are already up. Ted, I understand from the Sheriff's Office we already have an issue regarding your client?"

Looking across the table at his adversaries first and then to the judge, Ted spoke up, "Yes, Your Honor, I received a telephone call late yesterday evening from my client's doctor. Evidently, the day before yesterday, there was some kind of episode, and I have been informed it was medically impossible for Mr. Icovatti to travel. The psychiatrist does not want him to leave the institution right at this time. I have been assured this is just a temporary situation. My thought is it may take some time to get our jury impaneled, perhaps days, and the absence of the defendant at this stage of the proceedings is really not that crucial. Certainly the Court could address the issue with the venire right at the outset."

Delsander turned to the prosecutor, "Mike?"

"We have no problem with that, Your Honor."

"Very well then. I will address the issue right when we start. Gentlemen, I have no doubt in the future you will be asked about this day. I also have no doubt you will give it your all so that, no matter win or lose, you can look back and be satisfied you did your best. Please take your seats in the courtroom and we will get this thing underway." He rose and walked toward the closet where his robes hung. The "chapter" about Martin Delsander was about to begin...at least in the mind of Martin Delsander.

Voir Dire

Voir dire really was *not* an exercise in selecting the good jurors for your case; it was more an exercise in de-selecting the bad ones. But seasoned litigators recognized it as an even more important selection process; during voir dire many jurors selected which lawyer they were going to believe. The lawyer's initial impression on the panel during jury selection was that important.

Gerrity's method, not having engaged in the exercise for over six years, was quite "structured" (he worked off the list of questions he committed to his yellow legal pad) whereas Ted's approach was more conversational than anything else. He knew the jurors were "sizing up" the lawyers and he wanted them, above all else, to feel comfortable with him. He began to establish his credibility with them.

The whole process took the better part of five days and it was grueling. Only four jurors had been selected before the break for the weekend. Not only did they "burn" through the first one hundred and thirty-eight prospective jurors, another fifty needed to be called in order to seat the fourteen they needed. The issue, of course, was the pretrial publicity of the case. Truth be told, there probably wasn't a county or parish or whatever political subdivision in the entire nation that wouldn't have had this problem. The murder of this man had been the most noteworthy event in the entire world and for the better part of the year, it captivated television, radio, newsprint, and the internet. The irony for the attorneys is they didn't want a juror selected who had heard or seen too much, but if a prospective juror was honestly not familiar with the event, what hole had he or she been living in for the last year and how intelligent could he or she be? Delsander began the whole process by announcing to the venire the attorneys were hoping to seat jurors who were going to be fair and impartial but that was not Ted's goal, not even close; he wanted to pick jurors who would be sympathetic to Tony's plight.

Before day one of any trial, you have a general idea of what the evidence against you is going to be and what testimony you will have to rebut...but you can never know what will come out during the jury selection process. Many times, you ask a straightforward question... and you get a response out of left field. Ted had been involved in more than one case where an issue surfaced during jury selection and went on to become a major theme in the case effectively "derailing" the presentation Ted had been planning for months. Sometimes it happened to his opponent and that was good for him.

Early Wednesday afternoon, after the better part of four days (with a weekend sandwiched in between), they finally had their fourteen—six men and eight women. Of the fourteen, the defense team had ranked five as "high" (good for their case), four as "acceptable" and five as "risk." Juror Number One was a seventy-two-year-old Vietnam veteran and perhaps the leading candidate for foreman (if not "pulled from the jar" to be one of the alternates). The defense team would pay close attention to him during the presentation of the evidence. The panel included three other retirees, all with grandchildren; and one person with a medical background—an emergency room nurse. After they settled on their panel and the panel was sworn in, Delsander announced they were stopping for the day even though it was fairly early on Wednesday. He knew both the prosecution and the defense needed a break. He thought it best to start fresh with opening statements on Thursday morning. The defense team decided to get some rest and reconvene over dinner. Ted was already exhausted...even before opening statements and the presentation of the evidence would begin.

That evening they found a small, family-run spaghetti house on Cleveland's near west side. As they cleared the restaurant's vestibule, the aroma of garlic and cheese overwhelmed them...even before their eyes could adjust to the candle-lit dining room and before they could see the red and white checkered tablecloths and the big round basket-weaved bottles of Chianti on the shelves. They were hoping for anonymity, but when the owner's squat Italian wife wearing a white apron met them at the door, it was clear they would not have it. But they were representing Icovatti. She silently acknowledged them and waved her arm so they would follow her. She led them to a rather large booth at the back of the dining room right near the kitchen and out of sight of the other diners, one her family occupied twelve hours out of the day. She removed some papers and a calculator from the table and in Italian ordered her dark teenage daughter to wipe it off and get the silverware. Ted marveled at the woman and thanked her. She waved her hand in the air again and said in broken English, "We are open seven days. You come here whenever you want."

Ted began the discussion about the panel as soon as their bottle of wine was delivered to the table, before they even looked at the menu. "Well, it sure looks like we have a mixed bag. Happy with the older members and especially Mr. Noe, Number One. Don't think we have any 'law and order' types. What do you think, Mac?"

"We could have done worse. Number Six bothers me a bit, the one with the brother-in-law who is the cop. But overall, not too bad. Happy with the grandmothers. It will be interesting to see how they relate to Tony."

"What do you think, Mike?"

"Agree. I think the retired school teacher will do well for us. I watched her closely when Gerrity was up. I liked her responses. Noe is good, I agree."

"What about the other two Veterans?"

"Like them both," Mac replied. "The one, Webb, it appears has had some run-ins with law enforcement with her son, but I think that may work well for us."

Mike agreed.

The owner's wife approached with a large antipasto and a loaf of hot Italian garlic bread smothered with mozzarella cheese. She smiled at Ted when she put them on the table. "Mange, mange."

"Ted, I think you should defer your opening statement," Mac said.

Mike, rather than Ted, responded, "Why would we want to do that?"

Ted turned to him. "Mike, we've entered pleas of NOT GUILTY and NOT GUILTY BY REASON OF INSANITY. Mac thinks if we defer our opening, it puts us in a better position to determine our best avenue of attack, which way we'll need to go. There is even a small chance that after we hear their evidence we will maintain both defenses. By waiting, we afford ourselves the luxury of hearing all the State's witnesses before we have to make any decisions. We can then attack at their weakest point. I agree with Mac. I think deferring is definitely the way to go." Ted knew the "talking heads" would have a field day with this decision. Depending upon how things went, they could rip Ted apart. After all, unlike Ted, they enjoyed the luxury of hindsight.

Their delicious meals and the way they were received by this family of strangers buoyed their spirits. Two hours later they all got a hug on the way out. Mama Albertelli's would become Defense Headquarters.

Ted slept better than he expected that night.

Opening Statement

Thursday morning at 10:30 a.m., the courtroom was a bit different: guards at the door, electronics clearly present, hustle and bustle in Ratliff s courtroom next door, people crawling all over the 27th floor, especially the media. It was scary for everyone, even the lawyers. The chosen fourteen were already in the box and counsel was at their respective tables as everyone waited for the "Hear Ye, Hear Ye's." Tony Icovatti was still not in attendance.

Everyone stood when Judge Delsander swept into the room. He got right down to business, his manner dictating to everyone that he was in total control.

"Please sit. The record will reflect the jury has been duly impaneled and sworn in. Ladies and gentlemen, we convene here today to hear the case of *The State of Ohio vs. Anthony Icovatti*, aggravated murder. The attorneys have already been introduced to you. What happens next in the trial is the attorneys will give us their opening statements. Many judges describe opening statements as a 'roadmap.' The attorneys will be telling you what their case is, what they believe their evidence will show. It is a starting point for you. But what each side says in opening is not evidence and you are not to accept it as same. As I said, it is a statement of what each side believes the evidence in the case will be. Because the prosecution has the burden of proving their case beyond a reasonable doubt, they go first. The order of the presentation of these opening statements, as well as the evidence you will hear, does not mean one side is more important than the other. Someone necessarily has to go first and someone second. You must keep an open mind and not make any decision until the end of the trial, after you have heard all the evidence from both sides. Mr. Gerrity, you have the floor."

Gerrity took a deep breath. He had not been in this position in more than six years. Like riding a bike, he tried to assure himself. But...not really. Six years was a very long time and this was no ordinary bike; it had been labeled the "Trial of the Decade." He rose from counsel table and slowly strode to the podium, which stood fifteen feet in front of the jury box. He began slowly. "Your Honor, Mr.

Chase, ladies and gentlemen of the jury. May it please the Court. I stand before you as the representative of the people of the great State of Ohio."

Very good beginning, Ted thought to himself. *Just about everyone in the courtroom and certainly the jurors were "people of the great State of Ohio."*

"It is my task in this trial to prove to you beyond a reasonable doubt that Florida senator and presidential hopeful Alexander Chastain was murdered in cold blood not three blocks from this very courtroom...and that the murder was committed by a disgruntled veteran from Crawford, Ohio by the name of Anthony Icovatti.

"Our witnesses include an Iraqi war veteran by the name of Tim Neary; the Cuyahoga County Coroner, Abel Darmstadt; FBI Special Agent Gerard Penning, a gun shop owner from Crawford, Ohio by the name of Bobby Lee Burk; and a world-renowned psychiatrist from Johns Hopkins medical school, Dr. Frederick Hickman. Now...what are they going to say?

"First...Neary. Neary is a member of a group of veterans who, for the better part of a year, followed Chastain to his campaign stops. And why did they follow him? Because they despised Chastain and his politics. It was their goal to upstage the senator and disrupt his campaign appearances wherever and whenever possible. Tony Icovatti had been with the group for about four months before Chastain's murder...and he was a very active member. Neary will also tell us that at the crucial time the fatal shot was fired, the men were within a few hundred feet of Chastain...except for Icovatti. Icovatti was unaccounted for when the shot was fired. He was nowhere to be found.

"Abel Darmstadt, the County Coroner. Dr. Darmstadt performed the autopsy the day after the senator was shot. He ruled the death was a homicide. He extracted the fatal bullet from what was left of the senator's skull and provided that bullet to the FBI lab for testing. He will testify the fatal shot came from high above and to the right of the senator and this is consistent with where the murder weapon was found the next day…on the top deck of a parking garage about four city blocks from the stage.

"Gerald Penning, FBI Special Agent…an expert in weaponry. He conducted three different tests of the suspected murder weapon, a Remington M24 sniper rifle. What do those tests confirm for us? That this rifle was indeed the murder weapon. He will also testify that there was only one set of fingerprints on that rifle…and they belonged to the Defendant, Anthony Icovatti. Ladies and gentlemen, let me say that again. The evidence will show that there was only one set of fingerprints on the murder weapon, those of the Defendant.

"Bobby Lee Burk will testify that he has owned his gun shop in Icovatti's hometown of Crawford for over eight years. Three days before Chastain was murdered, he found an M24 sniper rifle was missing from his shop. The rear door to the shop had been pried open and the gun was missing. He will confirm through the serial number that the murder weapon was the very same gun taken from his shop.

"Now the State believes the defense will try to persuade you that Icovatti was not in his right mind when he did the deed—that he was, in fact, insane."

At this statement, the defense team exchanged glances.

"You will hear about his ordeal in Iraq and the loss of his best friend. This may cause you to have sympathy for him. But cases are decided on the facts and the law…not on sympathy. Dr. Frederick Hickman is a world-renowned psychiatrist at Johns Hopkins, one of the finest medical institutions, not only in our country but in the world. He examined the defendant, and he will tell us that Icovatti had the motive, the means, and the opportunity to do the deed and that he meticulously planned it out for weeks. Icovatti studied the senator. He tracked him. He even clipped magazine articles about him. He obtained a rifle in his hometown, and he carefully planned the assassination. Dr. Hickman will tell us this planning...this calculated design to do this thing...is proof beyond any doubt that Icovatti knew exactly what he was doing and that he is as sane as you or me. He was meticulous, ladies and gentlemen, and he was successful. He is, without a doubt, guilty of the murder of Alexander Chastain."

Gerrity returned to counsel table.

"Thank you, Mr. Gerrity," the judge said. "Mr. Chase, you have the floor."

Ted rose but did not move from behind counsel table. "Thank you, Your Honor. The defense defers its opening statement."

Ted threw the first "curve ball" of the trial and it was a good one, catching Gerrity off guard. But it unnerved Delsander a bit as well.

"Counsel, please approach the bench," he said stiffly.

When all four lawyers were at sidebar, Delsander addressed the defense. "You do not wish to address the jury at this time, Mr. Chase?"

"No, Your Honor. The defense defers its opening statement until the State has rested and the matter is turned over to the defense."

Gerrity looked troubled. He certainly hadn't anticipated this. *What has he got up his sleeve? I already told the jury that Chase would probably pursue an NGRI. If he doesn't, how will that make us look?*

"Very well. That is your option," the judge affirmed. "My thought today, since we got started a bit late, was that we would do openings and then let the jury have lunch. Mike, let's put your first witness on and then we'll see where we are. Please retake your seats."

He announced, "Ladies and gentlemen, the defense has exercised its option to wait to address you until we get to their side of the case. We are going to proceed directly to the presentation of evidence. Mr. Gerrity, please call your first witness."

Tim Neary

As soon as he received the trial subpoena, Tim Neary recognized that he was in a tight spot. He had been on the campaign trail every day for the better part of three months, drawing attention to the plight of America's veterans. Now the State was calling upon him to testify about Tony's sanity. The last thing he wanted to do was to help the government prosecute Tony Icovatti but...he had to tell the truth.

Neary could recall no mental health "episodes" when the men were together. It was seldom Tony discussed his time in Iraq, but when he did, he looked and sounded depressed. But they were all depressed when their thoughts turned to the atrocities they had witnessed and to their friends and fellow soldiers who did not return.

If asked, Neary would have to admit that Tony was not with them at the crucial moment in Cleveland when Chastain went down, that he and his friends had no idea where he was at the time. Neary also had a difficult time recalling how much time elapsed before Tony rejoined the group, that the ensuing pandemonium had "blurred" time. He realized that he was not going to be a good witness for his friend and fellow veteran, but he had no choice.

After Neary was called and took the oath, Gerrity began, "Mr. Neary, I understand you are a veteran of the second Iraqi conflict, is that right?"

"Yes."

"How many tours?"

"Two."

"Thank you for your service."

No response.

"Returned to the States after the second battle for Fallujah, am I right?" Gerrity continued.

"Yes, for treatment."

"For your injury?"

"That's right."

"And you have been discharged from the service?"

"Yes."

"Then at some time you formed a group and followed Senator Chastain?"

"No, I didn't form any group. I attended Chastain rallies with other like-minded veterans."

"I see. And for how long had you followed Chastain?"

"A little over a year."

"Do I understand correctly that Anthony Icovatti wasn't with you the entire year?"

"Only about three months. Met him on the way to Chicago."

"Tell the jury why you followed Chastain."

"Why did we follow him?" Neary asked, puzzled.

"Yes."

He shifted a bit in his chair so he could look directly at the jury rather than at Gerrity.

"Because veterans returning from Iraq and Afghanistan were being screwed and he made matters worse. We needed to counter his message."

"And that message was...?"

"Chastain failed to understand what we were doing over there. He believed our involvement there was wrong. He was an insult to those of us who went. He had no idea what he was talking about."

"An insult?" Gerrity poked.

"He maintained we were the aggressors in these countries and those who died did so without purpose. He was wrong."

"To your knowledge, did Anthony Icovatti share these beliefs?"

"Objection," Ted stood and interjected.

"Sustained," said the judge.

Gerrity had to figure another way to get this point across to the jury.

"Mr. Neary, did Anthony Icovatti participate in your group's activities at the Chastain rallies?"

"It wasn't my group, I already told you."

"Sorry. Did the defendant participate in the group's activities?"

"Yes."

"And at these rallies, what was it the group did?"

"We staged protests...tried to draw some of the media attention away from Chastain and to us."

"How would you do that?"

"We studied the location and tried to place ourselves where we could be seen, especially if there was television coverage. We would use bullhorns."

"And Icovatti was part of this?"

"Yes."

"Once the group arrived at the site of the rally, how were the decisions made about where to place yourselves and what to do?"

"We would approach it like a military objective, figure things out, try to give ourselves the best vantage point."

"Did Icovatti contribute to those discussions?"

"Sometimes."

"Did the group ever follow his recommendations?"

"Sometimes."

"He was arrested in Boise."

"That's right. Police really gave us a hard time there."

"What happened?"

"We wanted to set up in a certain place in a public park but they wouldn't let us. They started pushing and some of us pushed back."

"Icovatti?"

"Don't remember if he was involved in the pushing, but he was right there and the cops arrested everyone...so he went too. No big deal."

"Now I understand he did not travel with you to Cleveland."

"That's right."

"Tell me about that."

"Don't know what you mean. Tell you what? He did not go to Cleveland with us. He went home before we went to...Little Rock... I think it was. Said he would meet us when we got to Cleveland."

"Why didn't he go to Little Rock with you?"

"Said he was tired and just wanted to be home for a couple weeks."

"And did he meet you in Cleveland as he had planned?"

Ted didn't like the "as he had planned" part of that statement but it was not objectionable.

"He met us at the bus terminal."

"The Greyhound Bus terminal in Cleveland?"

"Yes."

"How did you get to the rally site from the terminal?"

"Walked."

"Did you figure out a good place to stage your demonstration?"

"Yes. On the steps of a building not far from the temporary stage."

"Was Icovatti with you the entire time?"

"He was with us all the way to the rally site and then I did not see him for a bit."

"Did he leave the group before or after Chastain arrived?"

"Before."

"How long was he gone?"

"I can't tell you. Don't really know."

"I mean was it ten minutes, twenty, a half hour?"

"Don't know and I'm not going to guess."

"Fair enough. How far from Chastain were you when the shot was fired?"

"About half the length of a football field."

"Fifty yards?"

"Give or take."

"Was Icovatti with you?"

"At the time of the shot, no."

"Did he re-join the group at some time?"

"Yes."

"How long after Chastain was shot did he re-join the group?"

"Can't tell you. Everything was going nuts at the time. Really have no idea."

"Did he say anything to you upon his return?"

"No, I didn't speak with him. The FBI agents were all over us fairly quickly and then they got Tony when he returned to the area."

"I understand each member of the group, including Tony, was questioned right here in this building and then let go."

"After a day or so."

"And then Tony was arrested the following week."

"That's what they tell me."

"In the three months Icovatti was with you, did he ever get in any arguments with you or the other members of the group?"

"Not that I recall."

"Pretty laid back, was he?"

"Not quite sure what you mean by 'laid back'...but he was alright, cool with everything."

"So no fights, arguments..."

"Not that I recall."

"Did you ever witness any irrational behavior from him?"

"Irrational? Not sure what you mean."

"In the entire time you spent with Icovatti, did you ever come to fear him in any way?"

"Fear him?"

"Yes. Because of anything he did or said, did he ever cause you to be afraid of him?"

"Afraid? No. Never."

"He was just one of the guys."

"That's right."

"Thank you. Mr. Chase may have some questions for you." Gerrity returned to counsel table and sat down.

Ted did not rise from his chair. Normally, during a cross examination, the seasoned lawyer wants the jury to focus on him rather than on the witness. During cross examination, the question is much more important than the answer. A good trial lawyer will always station himself "front and center" during cross examination. Some lawyers even made it a point to dress a little flashier when they knew they would have a long cross examination on a particular day of trial. But not in this case. Ted knew Neary was sympathetic, and he wanted the jury to really concentrate on Neary and his next round of answers. Ted wanted to become a part of the woodwork and *not* draw any attention to himself.

"Mr. Neary, you testified that Tony Icovatti met you at the bus terminal in Cleveland on the day of the rally," Ted asked, still seated.

"Yes."

"Do you know how Tony got to Cleveland?"

"Also bus."

"Any idea when Tony's bus arrived?"

"He had just gotten in. Said he arrived about fifteen minutes before we did."

"When you met Tony at the bus station before the rally, did he have anything with him?"

"Yes, he was carrying his small duffle."

"Anything else?"

"Not that I recall, just the duffle."

"You had seen this particular duffle bag before?"

"Yes."

"You said it was small, can you give us an idea?"

"Not much bigger than a backpack."

Ted got up, walked over to the table where the exhibits had been laid out, and picked up State's Exhibit 1, the M24.

"Mr. Neary, the government has marked this rifle as Exhibit 1 and they are telling us this is the murder weapon. Ever see this before?"

"Never."

"Could this rifle somehow fit into the duffle Tony had with him that morning in Cleveland?"

"No, it's impossible. Way too big."

"Even if it were somehow taken apart?"

"Well, just the barrel is longer than the duffle is wide. It would have had to stick out one way or another."

"When you met up with Tony in Cleveland, did you notice anything sticking out of his duffle?"

"No sir."

Ted returned the rifle to the table and re-took his seat.

"While he was with you, did you ever see Tony handle a firearm of any type?"

"No."

"Mr. Neary, any idea how long the group planned to remain in Cleveland after the Chastain rally?"

"We weren't staying. We were leaving that evening for Pittsburgh."

"Chastain's next stop?"

"Yes."

"Was Tony going with you?"

"Yes."

"How was the group getting to Pittsburgh?"

"By bus. We actually bought our tickets in Cleveland before the rally. They were cheap; Pittsburgh isn't far from Cleveland."

"Did Tony purchase a ticket to Pittsburgh?"

"Yes, we all did."

"So before the rally, Tony bought a bus ticket so he could see Chastain the next day in Pittsburgh."

"Yes."

A stirring from the back of the courtroom. Ted paused here for a good long time. Silence in the courtroom, not noise, gets everyone's attention. Gerrity was writing. Mac was hiding a bit of a smile. Mike now fully understood the decision to defer opening statement.

"So let me make sure I understand this," Ted picked up again. "Tony arrived before you did and he waited for you. You arrived about fifteen minutes later. Everyone, including Tony, bought a ticket for the trip to Pittsburgh and then you all walked to the Warehouse District where the stage had been set up for the rally?"

"Yes."

"Mr. Neary, when Tony was with you for that three-month period and the group had to walk anywhere, did he have trouble keeping up?"

"No. We made sure we didn't walk too fast."

"You adjusted your pace so Tony could keep up."

"Yes."

"Was the pace a bit slower than you would normally walk?"

"Yes, sir."

"Mr. Neary, showing you what the State has marked as Exhibit 8, I understand this is an aerial view of downtown Cleveland. I also understand the spot marked with an X is the parking garage where the murder weapon was eventually found. Will you take a look at this for a minute...I have some questions for you.

Neary took the blowup and studied it for about two minutes. He then looked up at Ted. "Okay."

"Tell me...when you walked to the sight of the rally, did you walk past the parking garage they have marked here by an X?"

Looking down, "Yes."

"And Tony was with you during this time?"

"Yes."

"And the entire group was walking a bit slower so Tony could keep up?"

"That's right."

"And the parking garage appears to be about four blocks from where the podium was set up? I believe they have the podium marked with a Y."

Neary looked down again at the blowup. "Looks that way."

"And during this time, Tony had nothing with him other than his small duffle bag?"

"That's right."

"Mr. Neary, what I want to discuss with you next is the distance between the bus terminal and the parking garage. And what I want to know is...do you think it would be possible for you, going at your normal pace, to walk from the Greyhound station to the parking garage, take the elevator to the highest deck of the garage, and once there, leave a weapon, return to street level, and then walk all the way back to the Greyhound station to meet your friends...and do it in less than fifteen minutes?"

"No. No way. It is too far."

"But I'm saying...at your normal pace?"

"I don't think I could do it if I were running. It's impossible. It's too far." Stirring from the back of the room. Gerrity was writing furiously.

"From your direct testimony, I understand Tony walked with you all the way to the warehouse district where the stage was set up and then he was gone for a time?"

"Yes."

"You didn't know where he was when the shot was fired."

"No."

"What about the other members of the group?"

"What about them?"

"Was anyone else missing at the time Chastain went down?"

"Couldn't tell you. Not my job to keep track of everyone."

"But that was the last time you were together with Tony?"

"Pretty much, yes. We were all separated when they did the questioning."

"Mr. Neary, for that three months Tony travelled with you, did you ever hear him voice any threats toward Senator Chastain?"

"No."

"Even as a joke?"

"No. None."

"Ever see him take any threatening action toward the senator in any of the venues?"

"No."

"To your knowledge, did Tony attempt to communicate with the senator in any way?"

"Communicate?"

"Talk with him, phone him, write to him...that sort of thing."

"Not that I know of."

"When Tony was arrested, he had a magazine article on his person of an interview with Chastain. Were you aware of that?"

"Yes. He had one article."

"That strike you as being out of the ordinary for someone interested in the senator?"

"Seeing as I had a folder full of articles on the guy, no."

"Did Tony ever discuss his service in Iraq?"

"Once or twice. He didn't like to talk about it...none of us did."

"Did he ever mention a soldier by the name of Salvatore Colonna?"

"Once."

"Have you ever seen Tony cry?"

"Yes, the one time he spoke of Colonna."

"Thank you, Mr. Neary."

"Any redirect, Mr. Gerrity?"

"No, Your Honor."

After Neary left the stand, Judge Delsander called the lawyers to the bench. "Gentlemen, it is a quarter to twelve. Mike, who is up next?"

"The County Coroner, Dr. Darmstadt."

"Ted, do you intend to cross the doctor at the conclusion of his direct?"

"Yes, Your Honor."

"Mike, then we have this Burk fellow?"

"Yes, Your Honor. But I have a message from my office that he called so I have to see what's up with that."

"Do you have your next witnesses available?"

"Yes, FBI Agent Penning and Dr. Hickman."

"Okay, let's send them out for lunch now and get them back by one-thirty and then we'll start back up with the coroner. How does that work for everyone?"

"I guess that would be okay."

"And you, Ted?"

"That would be fine."

"Ted, I understand from the Sheriff Mr. Icovatti will be joining us this afternoon?"

"Yes, Your Honor, I understand he's on the way."

"Fine then. Please return to your seats."

The judge looked across the court and addressed the jury.

"Ladies and gentlemen, we are going to break for lunch now. I understand arrangements have been made for you at Johnny's, a bit of a special treat. You will be escorted there by my bailiff and the sheriff's deputies. The Court will reconvene at one-thirty when we'll hear from the State's next witness. The bailiff will escort you back to the deliberation room. Please remember you are not to discuss the matter with anyone, even your fellow jurors."

"All rise!"

Everyone stood as the jury filed out, followed by Judge Delsander.

The defense team called ahead and then retreated to Mama Albertelli's. Mac was happy and Mike was almost giddy on the ride there. Ted, however, was thinking about the challenges to come: Darmstadt and especially Penning and Hickman.

Once they were situated in what had become "their" booth, Mike asked, "So why does Icovatti buy a ticket to see Chastain in Pittsburgh when he knows Chastain is not going to make it there? Is he that slick? I don't think so. And how does he get the weapon on the roof of the garage and get back to the terminal to meet Neary and the boys in under fifteen minutes...if an able-bodied man with two legs couldn't do it?"

"Good questions, Mike. Let's hope the jury is asking themselves the same ones," Mac said. Mac knew Ted did not want to discuss the morning that was over and done with. "Ted, you're all set for Penning? He is going to hammer the forensics, especially the fingerprints."

Before Ted could answer, Mike interrupted.

"I still don't understand how we get around the fingerprint evidence. Do we really have an answer for that?"

Ted's thoughts returned to his window cleaning at the cabin. "I have an idea but I'm not for sure. I have to be very careful with Penning on that issue."

Ted wanted to revisit the dual defenses the defense had asserted. "Mac, Neary did well for us and I do have some "zingers" for Penning, but I'm still not one hundred percent comfortable abandoning our insanity defense...not just yet. I've been on the phone to Berringer all week and Tony is not doing well at all. Believe it or not, this may be the first case where I'll continue to press both defenses, as much as I recognize pleading in the alternative usually does not fly with a jury. Any thoughts?"

"Well, if we're going to abandon the NGRI and put all our eggs in the 'NOT GUILTY basket,' Hickman's testimony becomes a lot less important to us. We really don't care about his opinion on Tony's sanity because we would be giving that point away anyway. The message from us would be...sure, he's sane, no one said anything different...but it does not matter because there is way too much doubt in the State's case—all those points Mike just brought up and whatever you can get out of Penning. That's your thinking?"

"Yes. But we lose one of our 'two bites at the apple.' If the jury doesn't see the evidence our way, we have no fallback position. Either one of you pick up anything from Noe?"

Mike responded, "No, not really, Mike responded. Bit of a stone face."

Mac shook his head. "Ted, conduct your cross examinations with the plan you will continue to press both defenses...at least for the time being."

"I agree. Probably the safest route for now."

Mama Albertelli was upset that they had called ahead and just ordered salads. She brought them a bowl of pasta anyway.

Back in Court

The rear doors opened and in walked a curious-looking character. He resembled a mad scientist: small in stature—not more than five-foot seven, white lab coat with a small bulge at the waist, bald head except for the sides, gray-white wispy hair sticking out in all directions...

matching eyebrows which were in serious need of a trim. He had a puggish nose supporting a twisted pair of pince-nez which sat crooked, reminding some folks in the courtroom of Cleveland's Mr. Jingeling of Halle's seventh floor. He kept both hands in the pockets of his lab coat, which appeared quite worn. After being sworn in and stating his name, he sat and waited for Gerrity. He was Dr. Abel Darmstadt, the county coroner for the last seventeen years.

Ted knew Gerrity would begin his questioning by establishing the doctor's medical credentials but there was really no need for that. Before J. Michael began, Ted stood.

"Your Honor, in the interest of saving time, the defense will stipulate to the qualifications of the witness and his fitness to render the opinion he was called here to give."

Delsander looked to the prosecutor, "Mr. Gerrity?"

Gerrity really wanted the jury to hear all about the doctor because, despite his diminutive stature and elf-like appearance, his education and accomplishments were impressive. However, Gerrity realized the jury would not appreciate him turning down his opponent's suggestion which would save time, and, from their point of view, some tedium.

"That would be fine, Your Honor." Turning to the witness, "Dr. Darmstadt, you are the Cuyahoga County Coroner and you performed the autopsy of Senator Alexander Chastain."

"Yes, right here in Cleveland the day after."

"Would you share with us how you go about that?"

"Certainly. The body is delivered to the morgue and the first thing we do is remove and catalogue everything we have—clothing, personal effects, jewelry. The corpse is tagged, weighed, and then a preliminary examination is conducted. We record our findings as we go along. Normally, after exsanguinating the remains, we would then make the appropriate incisions to expose and remove the essential organs: the lungs, heart, liver, brain. Those would be weighed and then examined for the presence of disease. However, there are times when that is not necessary due to the evident damage."

"Evident damage?"

"Yes. The task is to determine the cause of death. In this case, the back of the decedent's head was massively destroyed. A segment of what remained of the brain was actually exposed. You didn't need a medical degree to make the preliminary call. I concluded that there was no need to focus on organs other than the brain, or rather, what was left of it."

"Doctor, I am handing you a collection of photos collectively marked State's Exhibit 7. I believe there are twenty-five pictures. For the record, can you tell us what these are?"

"As we perform the examination, we record our findings via dictation but we also take photographs. These photographs document the findings of the autopsy."

"And the cause of death?"

"Homicide. A single, non-suicidal, gunshot wound to the back of the head causing massive destruction of the brain. All systems ceased. The heart stops, the lungs no longer contract, all major organs shut down. In this case...within less than two minutes."

"Did you retrieve any physical evidence from the corpse?"

"The bullet."

"Doctor, showing you what has been marked as State's Exhibit 2, can you tell us what this is?"

He examined the plastic evidence bag rather than its contents "Yes. This is the bullet I retrieved from the corpse. My notations are on the outside of the evidence bag to establish the chain of custody."

"This is the bullet that killed Alexander Chastain?"

"Yes, sir, it is."

"Do I understand correctly that after you retrieved this bullet from the body, it was sent to the FBI crime lab for testing?"

"That's correct."

"Doctor, from your investigation, were you able to determine the flight path of the bullet?"

"Somewhat. The greatest area of damage was to the back of the head just above the right ear. That area of the skull was totally destroyed as was a large portion of the brain. The bullet was retrieved from the left side of the skull, lower than the left ear. That indicated to me the shooter was somewhere behind and to the right of the senator. And judging from the downward angle, he was also at a higher elevation."

"So the shot came from above, behind, and to the right of Senator Chastain?"

"That would be accurate according to my determination."

"Doctor, showing you what has been marked as State's Exhibit 8. This is an aerial photo of the Warehouse District. The spot marked with an X is the parking garage where the rifle was found...on the roof...and the spot marked Y is where the podium was positioned for the rally. There is a red line drawn between the two marked spots, X and Y. Have you seen Exhibit 8 before today?"

"Yes."

"Is what you see here consistent with your opinion about the damage to the corpse and the direction of the fatal shot?"

"Yes. The roof deck of the parking garage appears to be behind, to the right, and higher than the location of the podium."

"Thank you, doctor. Mr. Chase may have some questions for you." Gerrity returned to his seat.

Ted waited a ten count before he rose. He walked over to the podium right in front of the jury. "Doctor, just a few questions. You offer an opinion on the cause of death but no opinion on who fired the fatal shot."

"That's correct. That's not what I was asked to do."

"Do you know of any evidence or testimony that places Tony on the roof deck of the garage at the precise time the fatal shot was fired?"

"No."

"What about at any other time?"

"On the rooftop?"

"Yes."

"No. I know of no such evidence."

"There is no evidence Tony Icovatti was to the right of the senator or to the left of the senator, higher than the senator or below the senator when the fatal shot was fired?"

"I know of none. That would be a question for someone else."

"Are you aware of any evidence of any nature regarding Tony's whereabouts at the time the fatal shot was fired?"

"No."

"Dr. Darmstadt, isn't it true that none of the evidence you discussed with Mr. Gerrity today really sheds any light on whether or not Tony Icovatti did anything."

"That's right. I was only called upon to determine the cause of death, not who did the deed."

"Thank you, doctor. I have nothing further."

Gerrity had no redirect. The FBI agent was up next.

FBI Agent Gerard Penning

Now here was an impressive-looking witness. FBI Agent Penning was a Marine veteran who returned from Vietnam in 1972 to complete his education at Northwestern's law school. He was sixty-four years' old and was nearing the end of his career as an agent for the Federal Bureau of Investigation. His expertise was in forensics, especially ballistics and prints. He was six foot two, still slender, with a full head of white hair, wire-rimmed glasses and sharp features. His suit was dark grey pinstriped, and his black shoes were like mirrors. He wore an American flag lapel pin. He was sworn in.

Gerrity started, "Agent Penning, for the record being made here today would you state your full name and spell your last name please?"

"Gerard Penning, P- E- N- N- I- N- G."

"You are an agent with the Federal Bureau of Investigation?"

"Yes, since 1976."

"Can you give the jury some idea of your education and training?"

"Certainly. I graduated cum laude from Loyola in Chicago. After graduation, I enlisted in the Marine Corps and went to Vietnam. Returned in 1972. I obtained my law degree from Northwestern and joined the Agency in 1976. After I joined the Agency, I underwent additional training in the field of forensics, specializing in weaponry."

"Ballistics?"

"Yes."

"Fingerprints?"

"Yes."

"And you were a member of the FBI team that investigated the murder of Senator Chastain?"

"That's correct."

"What was your role in the investigation?"

"I was called upon to perform an assessment of the M24, which was found on the roof deck of the parking garage here in Cleveland."

"From your previous military experience, did you have any familiarity with M24s?"

"Yes. For a time, a version of this weapon was standard military issue for use as a sniper rifle."

"Ever fire one before being called in on the Chastain investigation?"

"Several times."

Lifting the M24, Gerrity walked over to the witness. "Agent Penning, handing you what has been marked as State's Exhibit 1, can you identify this for us?"

He turned it over and looked closely at the white label attached by string to the trigger guard. He said, "Exhibit 1 is the M24 taken from the top deck of the parking garage."

"And how do you know it was this particular rifle?"

What followed was a lengthy discussion establishing the chain of custody of the murder weapon...from where it was found on the top deck of the Cleveland garage to the hands of Penning in the FBI lab.

"What testing, if any, was conducted on the rifle?" Gerrity asked.

"There were three separate tests. The first test was a dusting of the weapon for fingerprints. There was a test to determine gunshot residue. There was also a test to determine if the fatal bullet came from this M24."

"Let's start with a discussion of residue. What is that all about?"

"When a weapon is discharged, it is common that not all the powder ignites. Some of it is expelled back against the firearm and sometimes on the person or clothes of the shooter. If you can match up the powders, you may be able to tell who the shooter was. The test is usually more effective with handguns than rifles."

"How did the test come out in this case?"

"There was hardly any residue on the rifle. Not enough to even conduct a definitive test."

"So that was pretty much a dead end in this case?"

"Correct."

"And the test to determine if the fatal bullet came from the weapon?"

"Another bullet from the same weapon is discharged into a water tank where it can be retrieved without damage. What you have to understand is that each rifle barrel leaves distinctive grooves on the bullet. No two weapons leave the same grooves. The markings are so distinctive, they are often referred to as the 'fingerprint' of the weapon. The suspect bullet and the one retrieved from the tank are then placed side-by-side under a microscope and the markings are compared."

"And that was done in this case?"

"Yes."

"Showing you what has been marked as State's Exhibit 2, can you share with the jury what this is?" Gerrity handed him a plastic evidence bag containing the bullet that had been extracted from Chastain's head.

"This is the bullet which killed Senator Chastain."

"And how do you know that?"

"From the chain of custody as recorded on the outside of the evidence bag. The coroner removed this from Chastain's skull and it was transported to our lab for testing."

"Agent Penning, showing you what has been marked as State's Exhibit 3, can you share with us what this is?"

"Yes, this is the bullet I retrieved from the water tank within our lab. It was discharged from Exhibit 1."

"The M24 taken off the top deck of the parking garage."

"Yes."

"And 4 appears to be a collection of photographs marked 4-A through 4-L."

"Yes. I took twelve photos...what we saw when the bullets were compared under the microscope."

"A match?"

"Yes, a perfect match. There is no question: The bullet that killed Chastain came from the same rifle as the water tank bullet."

Holding up the M24, "State's Exhibit 1?"

"Yes, State's Exhibit 1 was the murder weapon. There is no question."

"Agent Penning, let's discuss serial numbers. Three days before the murder of Alexander Chastain, an M24 bearing serial number M04-1C-8241-24 was stolen from a gun shop in Anthony Icovatti's hometown. Did you determine the serial number of Exhibit 1, the M24 that fired the fatal bullet?

"Yes."

"And was it the same number as the rifle found missing from the gun shop in Crawford three days before Chastain's death?"

"It was the same: M04-1C-8241-24."

"The murder weapon, Exhibit 1, was at one time offered for sale in the gun shop in Icovatti's hometown and was found missing only days before the senator was murdered?"

"Yes."

"Were there any fingerprints on Exhibit 1?"

"One set."

"Showing you what has been marked as State's Exhibit 5, can you share with us what this is?"

"This is a transparency of the prints lifted from Exhibit 1 superimposed on the prints of the defendant."

"Icovatti's prints have been marked Exhibit 6?"

"Yes."

"So to compare them, the prints from the murder weapon are layered over top of the prints the FBI took from Anthony Icovatti once they had him in custody?"

"Yes."

"Results?"

"There is a perfect match. The fingerprints on the murder weapon are those of Anthony Icovatti."

"Any margin for error here?"

"No. None."

"Anyone else's fingerprints found on the weapon?"

"No."

"Were there any other substances found on the murder weapon?"

"Traces of alcohol."

"Did you find that unusual?"

"No."

"And why is that?"

"Almost all gun-cleaning solutions contain large concentrations of alcohol."

"It makes sense a rifle displayed in a gun shop would show traces of alcohol by virtue of it being readied for sale?"

"Absolutely."

Gerrity was all smiles. "Thank you, Agent Penning. I'll pass the witness."

Now it was Ted's turn. He returned to the podium and did not approach the witness box.

"Agent Penning, three forensic tests were conducted and two of them demonstrate no connection between the M24 and Corporal Icovatti, isn't that true?

"Not sure what you mean."

"The residue test was inconclusive on all counts; do I have that right?"

"Yes, that would be correct."

"And the water tank testing showed only the fatal bullet was discharged from the M24, but certainly casts no light upon who pulled the trigger."

"Yes, that is also true."

"The only evidence you offer today seemingly connecting the weapon to Tony is fingerprints."

"Yes, only his prints were on the weapon."

Ted walked over to the table holding the exhibits, picked up the M24 and was given permission from Delsander to approach the witness. Rather than handing the rifle to the witness however, he set it down in front of him on the railing of the witness box.

"Agent Penning, I am placing on the railing before you what the State marked as Exhibit 1, the M24. Can you hold the weapon in such a way to demonstrate to the jury the location of the fingerprints?"

He grabbed the weapon by its stock, lifted it from the railing, and appeared to aim it at the wall above the court reporter's head, away from the jury.

Ted stated, "The record should reflect that Agent Penning has placed the stock of the weapon in the crook of his right shoulder. His right hand is on the rifle near the trigger, with his right thumb curled around the top of the rifle and his right index finger on the trigger. His left hand is supporting the front of the M24's barrel from underneath.

This is the way such a rifle is usually aimed at a target, would you agree, Agent Penning?"

"Yes."

"Mr. Gerrity?"

"Yes."

"For the record, I am going to refer to that as the 'aiming position.' Ted took the rifle back from Penning.

"You testified there was only one set of prints on the weapon, and they were in the aiming position I just described for the record, am I right about that?"

"Yes."

"Well that doesn't make too much sense does it?"

"I don't see why not."

"When you picked up the rifle from the railing, you grabbed the weapon by its stock with your right hand, didn't you?"

Slowly..."Yes, I guess I did."

"When you conducted your testing, did you find any fingerprints on the rifle's stock?"

Slowly..."No."

Ted placed the weapon back on the railing. "Now, would you demonstrate to the jury how one would load the weapon? Please do it slowly so the jury can watch."

At this, Penning picked the sniper rifle up again and demonstrated how the weapon is loaded. Both of the agent's hands were all over it, not just in Ted's 'aiming position.'

"Agent Penning, forgive me, but it looks to me, from what you just showed us, in order to load the weapon, you placed your hands on the rifle in several places...not just where you detected the fingerprints. Would you agree with me on that?" Ted took the weapon back from the witness and slowly returned it to the table holding the exhibits.

No answer. Deep in thought.

Ted turned to the witness box "Do you understand the question, Agent?"

"Yes, I understood the question. You're wondering why there are not more prints on the weapon."

"And?"

"I don't have an answer for you."

"How does someone pick up the weapon and load it without leaving additional prints?"

"Like I said, I don't know."

"Thank you. I have no further questions." Ted returned to his seat at counsel table.

Gerrity was no longer smiling. *How did we miss this*?

"Any re-direct, Mr. Gerrity?" Delsander inquired

"Just one question, Your Honor. Agent Penning, did you find any evidence of any nature indicating a person other than Anthony Icovatti handled the murder weapon?"

"No."

"Thank you."

"Thank you, Agent Penning. You may step down," the judge said. "Mr. Gerrity, I understand Mr. Burk has been detained, and your next witness would be your doctor, am I right?"

"Yes, Your Honor."

"Very well then."

Frederick Hickman

Well-tanned. Twenty-five-hundred-dollar suit. Bruno Magli shoes. Tag Heuer on the wrist. Most expensive hairpiece on the market. You need an expert opinion on any type of psychiatric issue, Hickman was your man...for a price. He had been in more courtrooms than most lawyers. Some lawyers referred to men like him as "professional witnesses" while others just referred to them as "whores." He was sworn in and sat down.

Gerrity spent the first part of Hickman's direct exam establishing his credentials. Ted knew not to try to short cut Gerrity here. Truth be told, Hickman's education and practice in the field were unremarkable. His affiliation with Johns Hopkins was nothing more than a temporary assignment as an associate instructor...which had already ended. But, it was on his resume and he parlayed the connection into something much more than it really was. Ted had had run-ins with imposters like Hickman before.

Gerrity moved forward. "Dr. Hickman, you were called in on this case to evaluate the defendant, Anthony Icovatti, is that right?"

"That's correct."

"And this is not the first time you have consulted on a case in court."

"No, it is not."

"Please tell the jury how you go about it."

"Well, the first thing I do is take a history from the subject. May I refer to my notes?"

"Certainly."

Looking down at his report resting on the rail of the witness box and adjusting his glasses, Hickman read aloud. "Corporal Icovatti was injured while deployed to Iraq when his unit encountered an IED while on patrol near Sadr City."

"IED?"

"An improvised explosive device...more commonly referred to as a roadside bomb. They used to be called landmines."

"Okay."

"When the device detonated, he lost his left leg just above the knee, most of his left ear, and he sustained a severe head trauma which put him in a coma for the better part of two weeks. After being stabilized, he was flown to an Army hospital in Wiesbaden and then to Walter Reed here in the States. He underwent further treatment there, was fitted for a prosthesis and eventually returned home. Like many veterans returning from a war zone, he experienced some problems and eventually sought treatment with a Dr. Michael Berringer at a facility called St. Joseph's near his hometown of Crawford, Ohio. The diagnosis was PTSD and depression."

"PTSD?"

"Post-traumatic stress disorder. After being at St. Joseph's for a time, he left on his own volition and joined up with a group of veterans who were protesting against Senator Chastain. He followed Chastain for about three months as part of this group, took a week or two off and then met up with the group again in Cleveland on the day Chastain was murdered. He was arrested for the murder within a couple days."

"Did you ask him why he was following Chastain?"

"Yes. His exact words to me were, 'Chastain was full of shit.' Evidently, he disagreed with the senator's stance on America's involvement in Iraq."

"You mentioned post-traumatic stress disorder. Can you define that for the jury?"

"Certainly. PTSD was introduced into the third edition of the Diagnostic and Statistical Manual of Mental Disorders, the DSM III, in 1980. PTSD symptoms develop in the aftermath of trauma and can lead to new psychological, physiological, and behavioral patterns of reaction which were absent before the traumatic event. During World War II, it was simply referred to as 'shell shock' and, for the most part, was viewed as a weakness or even cowardice. But after Vietnam, it was studied more in depth and we came to understand much more about it. PTSD is a 'response to stress' syndrome that can vary in severity and intensity. A good example would be a veteran's overreaction to loud noises like the backfire of a car...because that would take him back to the war zone and remind him of incoming mortar rounds. It can govern behavior for years after coming home. Depression is often a significant component of PTSD."

"Icovatti was diagnosed with having PTSD and depression by Dr. Berringer?"

"Yes, he was."

"Was there more to the history you took from Icovatti?"

"Yes, I reviewed with him his family life prior to his enlistment, his education, occupational history and also his military experience prior to his deployment to the Middle East."

"Anything significant?"

"No. Not really. Very bright, did well in school. No major health issues prior to the injuries he sustained in Iraq. I think he had an emergency appendectomy when he was twelve. Nothing significant."

"Any prior legal problems or substance abuse problems?"

"No. Neither."

"After you took his history, what was the next part of your evaluation?"

"I conducted a mental status examination."

"Please share with us how you go about that."

"Well, you ask the subject to perform some simple mental exercises, answer some basic questions, and you observe. In Icovatti's case, he was cooperative and maintained fairly good eye contact. His affect appeared somewhat anxious and depressed, but he remained alert and oriented in all spheres. Immediate memory was intact for three out of three objects and for two out of three with a time delay with interfering tasks. Serial 7's both forward and backward were no problem for him. He could spell the word 'world' correctly forward and backward and he could name the months of the year in reverse order. Long-term memory was intact for the name of a childhood friend, elementary school teacher, and recent presidents. He correctly interpreted a proverb. The overall estimate of his intelligence was in the 'above average' range with current compromised focus, concentration, and calculation skills...but only to a small degree. He described his general mood as 'angry and depressed.' He indicated he had occasional nightmares about his service in Iraq that would awaken him and he sometimes experienced flashbacks...I think he indicated a frequency of about once a week. He acknowledged feeling depressed for most of the day and losing interest in many things that interested him before. He also expressed some measure of guilt about how his current condition affected the members of his family, especially his mother and father. He revealed that sometimes his anger and depression would rise to a level where he just wanted to shut out the world...just make it all go away. During those periods, he avoids people as well as places he used to enjoy. He reported decreased pleasure in certain activities he used to enjoy."

"Did you review any testing?"

"Yes, the MMPI and the Rorschach."

"MMPI?"

"The Minnesota Multiphasic Personality Inventory. It contains 567 true/false items that measure psychopathology and personality processes. It also contains validity indices that measure faking and malingering. The MMPI scales reflect the subject's attitudes and generate information revealing the mental state of the subject."

"And Rorschach?"

"The Rorschach is commonly referred to as the 'inkblot test.' Believe it or not, the inkblot test remains favored for assessing PTSD. The issue with the other testing, including the MMPI, is that the evaluator is forced to rely upon the self-reporting of the subject. Sometimes the vagaries or distortion of memory, and sometimes even downright manipulation of information, play a major role. In projective testing like the Rorschach, because the stimuli are ambiguous, the 'meaning' of any given answer could be unclear. But it is the collective response to the entire test that is important; no one answer carries that much importance by itself. There are no 'clues' within the test to guide the responses given. It is a truer assessment because it allows the evaluator to gain insight into the subject's inner experiences without having the subject address those directly. No issues with memory or deliberate misreporting."

"And you reviewed those results?"

"In depth."

"And what did you find?"

"The corporal does suffer from some degree of PTSD typically demonstrated by his avoidance of certain stimuli, hyper-reaction to other stimuli, and his loss of interest in activities he used to enjoy. He also has some depression. There is no doubt about that. However, for anyone to say his PTSD and depression rise to the level of insanity is psychological 'hogwash.' His degree of PTSD and depression are neither more nor less than almost every other veteran returning from a war zone. I take grave exception to any clinician who would offer an opinion that he was insane. In no way was Officer Icovatti robbed of his ability to know right from wrong...at any time."

"And do you hold this opinion with a degree of psychological probability or certainty?"

"Yes. There is no doubt about it. Anthony Icovatti has never been insane, not even for a short period of time...not remotely close."

Ted was thinking to himself, *this guy is polished*. Mac was tallying the points beginning to pile up against the home team.

"What, if anything, is there about Icovatti's conduct prior to the murder of the senator that supports your opinion, doctor?"

"The incredible amount of calculation and design to carry out his objective. First of all, we know he was actively gathering information about the senator, 'researching,' if you will. Then he made the conscious decision to join the group of veterans to make it easy to stalk the man...for months. The hiatus he took from his travels with the group in the two weeks or so leading up to the assassination indicates to me he was affording himself more time to plan. The rifle Icovatti used, stolen from a gun shop not two miles from his home just three days before, indicates to me he drew upon his military experience and knowledge of weaponry; he picked a rifle with a range of over half a mile. How and when he arrived in Cleveland, all alone and before he had to meet up with his buddies, tells me he thought that through; he needed to give himself enough time to set things up. He conveniently disappeared from the group at the time the fatal shot was executed and returned later without any degree of suspicion focused upon him.

And...more importantly, he was interrogated and released the next day...and not by some young Deputy Sheriff. He withstood hours of interrogation by the FBI's best...and he successfully convinced them all he had absolutely nothing to do with Chastain's murder."

Ted and Mac were sweating.

"He only made one mistake, is that right, Dr. Hickman?"

"That's correct. He left his prints on the weapon...the only prints on the weapon. Any mental health professional who evaluates these facts honestly and opines Icovatti was insane either doesn't know what he is talking about or is deliberately misdiagnosing. I suspect the latter in this case."

"Thank you, doctor. Mr. Chase may have some questions for you." Gerrity sat. Before Ted could reach the podium, there was a commotion at the rear of the courtroom.

Tony Shows Up for Court

Mike slowly opened the rear doors to the courtroom with his left arm, his right arm resting on the back of T's right shoulder to assist him. Even though the room was packed, it was dead quiet, all eyes trained on the entrance, all eyes except for Mac's. Mac's eyes never left the panel. The next few moments, Mac knew, would provide an open window into the hearts and minds of the fourteen people sitting in the box. When T came into sight, there was an audible gasp followed by a low "rumble." Judge Delsander used his gavel, but only once and not very hard.

The first thing the jury could see was the dirty, disheveled hair that ended raggedly on the left side of T's head exposing his scarred and reddened skull where hair no longer grew, just above the hideous protrusion of skin that used to be an ear. Five days growth covered his unwashed face and he had snot hanging from the end of his nose, which he wiped on his right forearm. He kept his left arm bent and his elbow tight against his side. He had one dirty, untied tennis shoe on his right foot and the shoelaces were dragging along the floor, but he had nothing on the end of his prosthesis as he shuffled, bent from the waist. He wore loose, stained sweatpants that used to be white and a heavily wrinkled, faded mustard colored T-shirt.

While keeping his body partially turned and his eyes fixed on the rear entrance, Gerrity, in a hesitant and uncertain manner, stood halfway up, his chair awkwardly scraping the courtroom's wooden floor, producing a screech. He dropped his pen, which fell part way under the table. "Your Honor..."

"Yes, Mr. Gerrity?"

Gerrity glanced at the jurors and then looked back at Mike and T and then turned his head toward the judge. He glanced down at the floor and the goddamn pen, bent down, picked it up, and then in a halting fashion, finally stood erect. His body language telegraphed his indecision.

"Your Honor..."

"Yes, Mr. Gerrity?" this time just a bit louder and sterner. "What is it?"

Delsander, too, was unprepared for Tony's arrival in this manner. Though not happy with what he was seeing, he exercised his "judicial restraint." He would not act on his own but would await an objection from the State. His mind raced about what ruling he would have to make in response while he waited to hear the word.

Ted was watching Gerrity out of the corner of his eye and was praying Judge Delsander would remain quiet. He knew his orchestration of

Tony's "grand entrance" (after taking care of himself—without help—for the last five days) was a calculated risk subject to an adverse ruling from the bench. Ted took the risk, however, knowing an instruction from the court could never erase from the jurors' memories the images of Tony that were undoubtedly being "burned" into them. Even if only brief, the jurors' view of Tony was more powerful than hours of testimony, providing better insight into what little was left of Tony's life.

Gerrity had been caught with his pants down. He overlooked the likelihood of Icovatti being presented to the jury in this way. He wanted to object but he couldn't think on his feet fast enough. He stammered a bit and his uncertainty about what to do was apparent to everyone. He told himself he should object. But wasn't the damage done? The eyes of each juror were fixed upon T from the moment Mike opened the courtroom doors. Would he be making it worse for his case by objecting? Should he ask for a sidebar conference and argue prejudice? What would happen then? Would the judge remove Tony from the courtroom? Would the jury hold that against Gerrity? Would they think Gerrity was trying to hide poor Tony from their view? But wasn't the panel now so compromised, the State could not receive a fair trial? He glanced at the jury, back at the door, and then to the floor again. His brain synapses were in meltdown.

"Mr. Gerrity, either say something or please sit down." Judge Delsander was not happy. Gerrity sat down and watched along with everyone else.

As soon as the doors had been opened, exposing the courtroom's parquet floor, Tony froze with a look of horror. His eyes became glued to the courtroom's center aisle. He took two steps forward, halted, then shuffled two steps to the left, halted again, then took one step forward. Then he froze again with a look of fright and confusion. He took another step forward and then moved sidewise three parquet blocks to the right, up against one of the pews. The lady sitting on that end quickly moved to her right to avoid being too close.

Mike looked to Ted for direction. At this rate, it was going to take Icovatti more than ten minutes to walk twenty-five feet to counsel table. Ted extended both arms with palms down sending the message to Mike, don't be concerned, just let him be.

The State's "star" psychiatrist, still sitting in the witness box, who was about to be cross-examined concerning the opinion he had just shared with the jury, began to fidget. He, too, looked at the floor as he felt his face begin to flush…and he hoped it did not show.

Ted was standing and had his back to Dr. Hickman, watching Icovatti's tedious trudge to the empty chair at counsel table. It seemed to take forever - which was just what Ted wanted. Tony moved like that video game character who had to avoid the little monsters trying to devour him with their sharp, munching teeth; one step forward, stop, two steps sideways, stop…

When Tony finally arrived at the table, perspiring and breathing heavily, Ted put an arm around him to settle him into the chair next to him. Tony immediately lowered his head onto his arms which he had folded on the table…so the jury could now see only the top of his head. Ted nodded toward the videographer, who put a life-sized picture on the monitor of an incredibly good-looking, smiling Tony wearing his dress uniform. The two older female jurors wiped their eyes and several of the jurors shifted in their seats.

Ted turned around to the witness.

"Doctor Hickman, did you just witness the defendant in this case, Corporal Anthony Icovatti, enter the courtroom and proceed to his seat at counsel table?"

"Yes," he answered, with a small gulp.

"Did you witness the manner in which he did that?"

"Yes."

"Do you know why he walked in the manner that he did?"

"I think I may know."

"And would you share that with us, doctor?"

"He was avoiding IEDs."

"Roadside bombs."

"Yes."

In this short time, T had raised his head from his arms folded on the table and began rocking back and forth in his chair. He kept his head tilted and his seemingly "dead" eyes staring blankly downward. He was muttering quietly, almost like a chant: "Died in vain...died in vain...died in vain...died in vain...." It started as a whimper but grew quicker and louder with every "incantation." Ted had to stop his questioning of the State's star witness. The jury was no longer listening because their eyes were fastened upon Tony. As Ted retreated to counsel table to try to calm him down, Tony suddenly jumped from his seat and yelled as loud as he could, "No! He didn't die in vain! He didn't die in vain!" Then he collapsed into his chair and started to cry, and the rocking back and forth resumed, now more violently.

Ted motioned to Mike, who looked for help from the bailiff, and the two men escorted the weeping defendant from the courtroom arm-in-arm. He offered no resistance.

Judge Delsander said, "The record should reflect that the defendant has been removed from the courtroom. Mr. Chase, please continue." *And thank God*, the judge thought to himself. The State had offered no objection to Ted's ruse, so no need for a ruling, and the defendant was no longer present.

Good trial lawyers like Ted are adept at thinking on their feet. Given Tony's outburst, he immediately recognized an opportunity to drive a significant point home with the jury. Ted walked over to the videographer and instructed him to roll a certain video. Alexander Chastain's handsome visage with the blonde hair and the pearly white teeth filled the screen. The voice was that of Carson Nelson. "Senator, if I understand you correctly, you're saying our involvement in Korea, Vietnam, Iraq, and Afghanistan were all major mistakes."

"That's right, Carson."

"And the tens of thousands of Americans who lost their lives in those conflicts—"

Chastain did not let him finish his question. "They died in vain, Carson, every one of them. They died in vain; we learned nothing. We repeated the mistake over and over again."

The screen went blank. Ted turned to the witness.

"Doctor, did you hear what Tony shouted before he was taken from the courtroom?"

"Yes."

"Did you recognize the face on the video which was just played for the jury?"

"Yes."

"Part of an interview with Senator Chastain."

"Yes."

"And you heard what he said?"

"Yes."

"Do you know who Tony was referring to a few minutes ago when he yelled out, 'He didn't die in vain?'"

"I think so."

"Who was he referring to?"

"A soldier by the name of Salvatore Colonna. They were friends."

"Lifelong friends."

"Yes, that is my understanding."

"They joined the service together."

"Yes."

"Colonna died in Iraq."

"That's correct."

"Do you know how?"

"Yes, a roadside bomb."

"An IED."

"Yes, an IED."

"The same bomb that caused Tony's injuries."

"I believe that's right."

"Tony lost his left leg and his left ear and part of his scalp. He was in a coma for almost two weeks."

"He sustained a major head injury...and...the amputations."

"He sustained a major head injury because he was hit in the face by Colonna's helmet. Isn't that true?" Ted asked.

"Yes."

"Do you know what was inside Colonna's helmet?"

At this question, the witness shifted in his seat and stifled a small cough with his rolled up right hand. He coughed again....then weakly, quietly said, "His head."

"I'm sorry, doctor, I didn't hear you. Can you speak up a bit?"

Hickman flashed a momentary look of anger at Ted, who was forcing him to repeat something he was loath to say....and he overreacted. "His head! Colonna's head was severed. It was still in his helmet, Counselor." *Screw you.*

The face of every juror reflected horror. Every juror. There was another audible gasp from the courtroom, which was now stirring. The judge banged his gavel twice but not loudly. *Why did Gerrity leave this out?*

"That's correct, doctor. And do you know what happened to the remainder of Colonna's body?"

"Yes."

"Would you share that with us, doctor?"

"The bomb pulverized his body," he replied. "There was nothing left, just the head." *Why did Gerrity leave this out?*

The stirring grew into a low rumble...met with a sharp gavel strike immediately silencing the room. Ted waited for ten seconds to pose his next question, which he knew would seem like an eternity. He also knew this brief silence would draw even greater attention to what was to follow.

"Doctor, when a psychiatrist is conducting an evaluation in order to arrive at a diagnosis, how important is it for the doctor to have the accurate history of the patient?"

"Extremely important," Hickman replied, regaining his composure.

"Why?"

"Because there are multiple psychiatric conditions or sicknesses, if you will, and many are closely related. You need to have all the factors to be certain of what you're dealing with...the treatments may be markedly different." *Chew on that, Counselor.*

"All the factors?"

"Yes, sir."

"Doctor, were you aware that it was Tony who talked his best friend Sal into joining the military?"

The doctor hoped he didn't hear what he just heard; he needed additional time. "I'm sorry, will you repeat the question?"

"Did you know Salvatore Colonna had second thoughts about military service but it was Tony who convinced him to join? I didn't see any reference to that in your report."

With a side glance toward Gerrity, "No, I didn't know."

Ted feigned surprise and offered a statement rather than a question. "You didn't know that."

"No, that information was not given to me."

"That was an important factor, wouldn't you think?"

"Well...," Hickman needed more time. He was making the classic mistake of trying to figure out where his interrogator was going with his line of questioning instead of just telling the truth.

"When you formed the opinion you just gave to Mr. Gerrity here...'within psychological probability or certainty,' that's how you said it, right...'within psychological probability or certainty'?"

"Yes, that's correct."

"When you formed your opinion 'within psychological probability or certainty,' it is fair to say that you took into account Tony's grief at losing his best friend?"

"Yes."

"Grief would be an expected response to such a loss."

"Yes."

"But when you formed your opinion, doctor, isn't it also fair to say that you gave no consideration to Tony's feelings of responsibility for the death of his lifelong friend?"

"No...I did not."

"What about fault?"

"No."

"Blameworthiness?"

"No."

"Culpability?"

"No."

"Guilt?"

"No."

"Regret?"

"No."

After each answer, Hickman glanced sternly at Gerrity. With each admission, the opinion the expert had just offered was slowly eroding but it was not the doctor's fault; Gerrity had failed to share with him this very key fact. Color was beginning to climb up the doctor's neck.

Ted waited another ten seconds, bowing his head as if deep in thought pondering his next question. But he already knew what his next question would be; he had been there many times before. He slowly walked away from the doctor, head still bowed, and stood right in front of Gerrity, looking down at him with his back to the witness stand. Ted spoke up, still facing the prosecutor rather than the witness "Doctor, in all fairness to you, you could not factor in these feelings or emotions when you arrived at your opinion because this one key fact was not provided to you, isn't that correct?" Ted knew the answer to this question would allow the jury to respect the witness and his credentials but still reject his opinion.

The doctor could not say "Yes" soon enough or loud enough. He was "defending" himself.

Slowly turning back around toward Hickman, Ted said to him, "Doctor, will you admit to this jury you would have liked to have known that fact *before* you rendered your opinion?"

Quietly, "Yes."

"I'm sorry, doctor, I did not hear your last answer."

Gruffly, "Yes, I would like to have known that." *Gerrity, you jerk.*

Most lawyers would make the mistake of asking the next question about how this very important missing fact would have affected the doctor's opinion regarding Tony's sanity, but Ted knew better. Ted knew that question would present Hickman an opportunity to explain it all away and "rehabilitate" his opinion...and he wasn't about to let that happen. Ted now had a "gem" to argue to the jury in closing and he wasn't letting anyone "tarnish" it: Remember, ladies and gentlemen of the jury, the State's psychiatric expert, Dr. Hickman, admitted from this very stand that he was not given all the information he needed before he rendered his opinion...a very important fact was not shared with him...and he wanted that information."

Hickman's mind, however, was in light speed formulating an answer to that very obvious question because he was sure Ted was going to ask it. Once again, he was anticipating the direction of his interrogator, so was caught a bit off guard by Ted's next question, a simple one.

"Doctor Hickman, Doctor Berringer is going to be called to testify on Tony's behalf, you are aware of that?"

Hesitating. "Yes."

"Do you know how long Tony has been under his care?"

"Off and on, I believe, for about fourteen months," he said slowly. *Where was this going?*

"And during that fourteen-month period how many sessions did Dr. Berringer conduct with Tony?"

"I really don't know. You would have to ask him." *Screw you.*

"Your Honor, may counsel approach the witness?"

Delsander nodded. Hickman shifted in his seat. *Now what?*

Ted grabbed a black three-ring binder from counsel table and walked up to the stand.

"Doctor, I'm handing you Dr. Berringer's treatment chart. You reviewed this chart, did you not?"

"Yes."

"Please turn to the last page of the chart and tell the jury the number of sessions Dr. Berringer conducted with Tony."

He took the records from Ted...only because he had no choice... and his reluctance was apparent to the jury. He opened the binder, glanced at the last page of the record, flipped the binder closed and said, "Looks like thirty-three."

"Now tell the jury how many visits you had with Tony."

Hickman needed to dodge this one because he knew where Ted was going...but…too late.

"Well…Counselor, you need to understand something. I was not..."

Ted cut him off. He could not let the witness try to control the examination. "I understand perfectly, Doctor. Is there something about the question you don't understand? It is a straightforward question."

"I understand the question, Counselor." *You asshole.*

"Please answer it then."

"One. One visit."

Ted picked up his copy of Hickman's written evaluation of Tony. "Says right here your one interview with Tony lasted about an hour and ten minutes. That correct?"

"Yes."

"Did you interview his parents?"

"No."

"Did you observe Tony in any other setting?"

"No."

"Did you conduct your own psychiatric testing?"

"No."

"Did you ever have to consider any medications for Tony at any time?"

"No. I wasn't the treating physician, Counselor."

"That's right. You weren't. Dr. Berringer was."

No response. No acknowledgement.

Ted wanted Hickman to admit it out loud. "Dr. Berringer was Tony's treating physician, isn't that correct, doctor...for fourteen months?"

"Yes."

"And he remains his treating physician."

"Yes."

"So tell the jury who knows Tony better: you, who met with Tony once for about seventy minutes...or Dr. Berringer who has been treating him for more than a year and continues to treat him today." Ted did not care how Hickman answered because he had him both ways. He tells the truth and says "Dr. Berringer," and it is a huge admission. He lies and says "I do," and the jury discounts all his testimony because the answer is simply not believable.

"Objection!"

Even better, thought Ted. Gerrity just telegraphed to the jury he was afraid of the answer and wanted to keep it from them.

Before Delsander could rule on the objection, Ted said: "Your Honor, I'll withdraw the question. I think everyone in the courtroom already knows the answer anyway."

"Objection!"

"Mr. Gerrity, there was no question for you to object to. Mr. Chase, please keep your comments to yourself."

"Yes, Your Honor."

Ted took the medical chart back from Hickman and very slowly returned to counsel table and set it down. He glanced down at Mac and then very slowly turned to face the witness. He waited, he bowed his head down, and slowly raised his right hand to support his chin. His eyes were closed, giving the appearance he was in deep contemplation. He waited. The dead quiet of the room was interrupted only by a singular cough from the back pew...which significantly underscored the stillness. He waited some more.

Then he pierced the silence, "Doctor Hickman...one last question."

Hickman shifted forward in his seat and he concentrated with all his intensity. He, along with everyone else in the courtroom, recognized an attempted "knockout punch" was on the way. He had to deflect it.

Ted waited a ten count more and then slowly asked, "Does a sane man fear there are landmines planted in the floor of a courtroom?"

The witness bowed his head, if just for a second or two. Defeat; for there could only be one answer. Quietly, "No."

"Thank you, doctor. No further questions."

Mac was using his left hand to cover his mouth and chin to conceal his smile from the jury as he scrutinized their body language. If only we could stop the proceedings now and let them decide, he thought to himself, for he knew in order to find guilt, the jury had to buy into Hickman's opinion that Tony was sane. Given the doctor's performance, Mac was certain they could not. What had seemed so "dead certain" a short time ago during direct examination...was now gone. But what was Gerrity going to do on re-direct?

As soon as Ted sat down, J. Michael was on his feet but...he had a problem. His key witness had just been filleted, was *not* in a good mood, and wanted off the stand and out of the courthouse as soon as possible. In previous high-profile cases, Hickman had gone toe-to-toe with some of the nation's best litigators...and did well. But here, in the biggest case he had ever been in, playing out before the world, he had been diced up by this country bumpkin. Hickman was madder at Gerrity than he was at Ted.

To his credit, J. Michael appreciated Hickman's current mindset, but he could not let Ted's cross-examination go unchallenged. He decided to stay on the outside and not wade in too deep, now fearful of Hickman's present frame of mind...and not knowing what he might say.

"Dr. Hickman, I have just one question. Did any of the questions put to you by Mr. Chase change your opinion about the defendant's sanity?"

"No."

"Thank you, doctor." And Gerrity sat down.

Nice try, Mac thought to himself, *but totally ineffective.*

Hickman bolted from the stand, his face and neck glowing.

"Ladies and gentlemen, it's after five and we are stopping for the day. Please remember the instructions given to you regarding your conduct during the pendency of the case and that you cannot discuss the case with anyone...including your fellow jurors. Please be back in the jury room at 9 a.m. tomorrow morning. The bailiff will escort you out."

"All rise!"

The jury filed out of the box one by one, followed by Judge Delsander.

What the jury was taking home with them—the last thing they saw and heard—was the State's "star" witness falling flat on his face. Regardless of Delsander's instruction to the jurors at the outset of the trial that they must "wait until all the evidence is in before reaching a decision," both Ted and Mac believed many of them would decide the case for themselves that evening.

Gerrity did not comprehend what he had just done. After the doctor's cross-examination, any juror possibly "leaning" toward a finding of sanity at this stage in the proceeding would be expecting Gerrity to "restore" Hickman in some way; it was absolutely necessary. When Gerrity failed to do so, he lost considerable ground with the panel because no juror could "champion" Hickman's opinion with their fellow jurors. It simply was not possible.

Lawyers trying cases oftentimes lose sight of this dynamic. The lawyer cannot enter the jury room nor take any role in the jury's deliberation. In every close case, the deliberations begin with the jury being divided. In order to carry the day, the lawyer must have advocates in that room—jurors willing to go to bat for the position the lawyer is advocating. In Tony's case, any juror leaning toward conviction must have the ammunition to defeat an insanity finding...but Hickman and Gerrity failed to give that to them. Hickman had admitted Tony's courtroom conduct was that of an insane man...and Gerrity's weak rebuttal did not overcome it. Mac knew any juror leaning toward conviction at this stage of the trial would feel "betrayed."

"I'm just going back to the hotel to take a hot shower and unwind," Ted said. "How about I meet you and Mike at Mama Albertelli's for dinner about eight or so? Let's get our booth in the back corner where we can eat and talk in private."

Mac looked at Mike and nodded.

Ted stood in the hot shower for half an hour trying not to relive the events of the day. If there is one thing Mac taught him, it is once a day of trial is over, it is over, and there is absolutely nothing to be gained by looking back upon it and figuring out what you might have done differently or better. Another thing Mac had taught him was that there's nothing more effective than for the defense to establish reasonable doubt with the State's own witnesses. Mac's smile had confirmed that he had accomplished that today with the State's most important witness. He threw on a bathrobe, laid down on the bed, and gave Dorie a call.

That evening, Mama Albertelli's was even better than their first visit.

Friday Morning

Bobby Lee arrived at the Justice Center very early. It was Gerrity's original intention to put him on the stand Thursday afternoon and save Hickman for last on Friday. That didn't happen because Carrie had taken a turn for the worse Wednesday evening and Berringer wanted Burk at her side. He was excused from appearing until Friday morning. Having Burk go last may have worked out well for the prosecution. Perhaps it was better to end with Burk testifying about how the murder weapon was stolen from a gun shop in Icovatti's hometown just three days before the murder.

After the jury and the judge were seated, Bobby Lee was sworn in and took the witness stand. But even if Burk did well, after Hickman's performance, Gerrity realized he had damn well better score some major points against the defense's psychiatrist Dr. Berringer.

First, Gerrity discussed Bobby Lee's background with him, including his military service, marital status, and length of time as a resident of Crawford. Then he got down to a discussion of the missing rifle. Burk testified in a very confident manner.

"Mr. Burk, for the record, I'm handing you State's Exhibit 1, which has already been established as the murder weapon in this case. Please take a few minutes to look at it as I have some questions for you."

Receiving the weapon from Gerrity, but really taking no time at all, Burk said, "Okay."

"Earlier in the trial, I represented to everyone that Exhibit 1 was the M24 that was stolen from your gun shop. Three days before Senator Chastain was murdered, was your shop in Crawford, Ohio broken into?"

"Yes, sir. The back door to the shop was busted open."

"Was anything taken from the shop?"

"Yes sir. An M24 which I had displayed on the center display case."

"Is Exhibit 1 one that same weapon?"

After taking a couple of seconds to look at the serial number, Burk replied, "Yes, sir. It is."

"And you know this from looking at the serial number."

"Yes sir, right here: M04-1C-8241-24." Burk was pointing.

"Did you ever have to check that number against your inventory?"

"Yes, sir, at the request of the Crawford Police."

"Who were investigating the theft."

"Yes, sir."

"Was anything else taken from the shop?"

"Not to my knowledge. At least no other weapons were taken. Whether or not some ammo was missing, I really couldn't tell you. We don't keep that close 'a record. We have over a thousand boxes of ammunition in the shop. If any ammo went missing, that would only show up when we take inventory at the end of the year."

"But just to be sure, the rifle you are holding, State's Exhibit Number 1, was definitely in your shop for sale up until three days before the senator was assassinated?"

"Yes, sir. I'm certain of it."

"How did Crawford's investigation of the theft turn out?"

"Nothing came of it until they got a call from the authorities here in Cleveland."

"After Senator Chastain was murdered."

"That's right."

"Mr. Burk, to your knowledge, are there any other stores in Crawford where one could obtain a rifle like this, an M24?"

"There are no other gun shops but there is a Wal-Mart that has a small selection of firearms. That's about it. They don't carry rifles like this one, though. This is a very special unit. Too expensive for Wal-Mart."

"And you know this how?"

"Well, they're really my only competition, a little bit anyway, so I keep an eye on what they offer for sale and on their pricing."

"Mr. Burk, prior to Chastain's death, had you ever met Tony Icovatti?"

"No, I never met him. But I had seen him at St. Joseph's when I went to visit there."

"What is St. Joseph's?"

"A rehab facility in Crawford, Ohio."

"The same town as your gun shop."

"That's right. My hometown."

"Anthony Icovatti's hometown?"

"That's what I understand."

"Icovatti and the person you were visiting were residents of St. Joseph's at the same time?"

"Yes, for a time they were. And I saw him there."

"Ever speak with him?"

"No, sir. Kind of keep to myself when I go there."

"To your knowledge, was Tony Icovatti ever in your shop prior to Chastain's murder?"

"Honestly, I can't be one hundred percent on that. I have friends who cover for me when I have to run errands. If he bought something, there would be papers on it. If he didn't, no way of tellin'."

"Did you look for any papers relating to the defendant?"

"Yes, sir. You asked me to."

"Find anything?"

"No, sir."

"In the week before the M24 went missing, was there a time when you had to be gone from the shop and you had someone cover for you?" This was an important fact for Gerrity to establish because it planted the seed that Icovatti might have been in the shop without Burk's knowledge. Bobby Lee made it sound like he would, from time to time, ask someone to watch the shop for him as a favor. But the truth was he had one employee who worked part-time and was paid under the table—not something Bobby Lee was about to share with anyone, especially here in court.

"Could be. It's possible. Don't really keep track of that."

"Mr. Burk, I understand Exhibit 1 had traces of alcohol on it when it was found. Can you explain that to me?"

"Sure. When I put a gun on display, I want to make it look as good as I can so I clean them all before I put 'em out there. Cleaning solution."

"The solution used to clean guns has alcohol in it?"

"Yes, sir."

"So the fact that the rifle had traces of alcohol on it is nothing out of the ordinary?"

"No, sir. I'm sure just about every firearm I have on display would have it, too."

"Ever have a break-in at the shop before this one?"

"No, sir. First one…and last one, I hope."

"Thank you, Mr. Burk. Mr. Chase may have some questions for you now." Gerrity returned to his seat.

Delsander spoke up, "Thank you, Mr. Gerrity. Your witness, Mr. Chase."

Ted's mind turned to window cleaning at the cottage but before Ted could rise to his feet, the courtroom doors opened and one of the Deputy Sheriffs who had been standing guard outside in the hall entered.

Delsander looked up, a bit annoyed. "What is it, Deputy?"

"Your Honor, may I approach the bench?"

"Yes. Come over to this side, over here by the court reporter."

Delsander cautioned the young Deputy Sheriff to keep his voice down.

He whispered: "Your Honor, there has been a threat to the building and I have been ordered to get this floor evacuated."

"Wait just a second, Deputy." Looking out at the lawyers, Delsander said, "Will counsel please approach the bench."

With all four attorneys up there, the sidebar conference looked more like a football huddle.

"Go ahead, Deputy."

"There has been a threat to the building and I need to get this floor evacuated."

"The whole building is to be evacuated?"

"Yes, Your Honor."

"Any idea what we may be looking at time-wise?"

"Your Honor, there are almost two thousand people presently in the building and we need to get everyone out. That alone is going to take quite a bit of time. The elevators are going to be shut down."

"No elevators?"

"No, Your Honor. Everyone is going to have to use the stairwells. There really is no way to tell how long it will take, could be the better part of the day before everything gets checked out. They're bringing the dogs over now."

Delsander's concern was evident. He looked at the lawyers. "Gentlemen, my first thought is for our jury. We have a lot invested in them by now and the last thing I want is for them to be compromised in any way. Also, unless I know for sure we are going to be back at it today, my inclination is to just stop everything right now and come back next week."

"Your Honor, Monday is a federal holiday," Gerrity said.

"Yes, I am aware. I'm sure you gentlemen can use the break."

"But we have the jury sequestered. Once they leave here this morning, they'll be holed up for almost four days."

"I am aware of that as well," the judge responded. "Here is what I plan to do."

Looking at the young man, "Deputy, this jury cannot leave the building using a stairwell with everyone else. This building is crawling with spectators, the media, criminal defendants, and God knows who else. They cannot be exposed to that. Lord only knows what they might hear. You are going to take them back to the deliberation room where they can gather their things and then you are going to take them to the bank of judges' elevators in the private hallway behind chambers. Take them down by elevator and then get some help and escort them to their rooms at the Marriot."

Looking at the lawyers, "As for the long weekend," the judge looked back at the lawyers, "the jury was facing that anyway. The only additional time involved is because we have to stop so early today. Gentlemen, any thoughts, objections?"

No one came up with anything.

"Alright then. Please return to your seats. Deputy, you stay right here."

When the lawyers reached their tables, Delsander spoke to the courtroom.

"Ladies and gentlemen, the deputy here has informed me some moron has made some sort of threat against the building. I am sure it is nonsense and we have nothing to be worried about.

However, out of caution, the building is being evacuated, and it may take quite a bit of time before we can resume, if at all, today. I have elected to stop the proceedings now and reconvene Tuesday morning after the holiday."

A collective groan rose from the courtroom.

"Yes, I know," the judge responded. "The other thing I hate to tell you is we are going to have to exit the building via the stairwells as the elevators need to be shut down."

(Louder groan.) "Please understand these precautions are for your safety."

Looking down at Burk, who had not left the witness box, the judge stated: "Mr. Burk, I am sorry, but you remain under subpoena, so I need to have you back here Tuesday morning by 10 a.m."

Burk responded, "That's no problem, Judge."

"Very well then." Delsander stood up and so did everyone else in the courtroom. Leaning over, he whispered to the deputy, "Take them by elevator and make sure no one communicates with them. Anyone says anything, you report to me."

"Yes, sir."

"Ladies and gentlemen of the jury, please follow the deputy here. He will see to it that you return to your hotel. Counsel, a very quick meeting in chambers and then we'll get you out of here."

The courtroom emptied.

Back in chambers, Delsander addressed the lawyers. "Well...just when you thought you've seen it all..."

They chuckled.

"Okay...let's talk about Tuesday morning. Ted will cross Burk first thing, is that right, Ted?"

"Yes, Your Honor."

"Mike, what else are we looking at?"

"After Burk, the State will rest."

"Fine. Do I understand there have been no objections to the State's exhibits, Ted?"

"Correct, Your Honor. No objections."

"Okay. We will address all the exhibits at the close of Ted's case. After Ted is done with Burk, we'll go right to Ted's opening and follow that with Ted's first witness. Everyone okay with that? This threat nonsense has set us back a day."

No one had any objections.

"Very well then, I guess we all need to get the hell outa' here before we all get 'blowed' up."

Chuckle.

Burk's Gun Shop

On the drive back to Crawford, Ted, Mac, and Mike discussed the day's events and how they believed they had fared. They were very upbeat, given Hickman's poor performance. The general consensus was an NGRI finding was looking good. But Ted had a hunch about Burk—he wasn't satisfied he had the entire story. When they arrived at their office in Crawford, Ted said, "Mac, Mike, tomorrow afternoon I'm goin' up to the cottage with Dorie for the long weekend—collect my thoughts and get ready for Tuesday. If you need me for anything or have any thoughts, call my cell and I'll do the same. I have one stop to make on the way up. Should be at the cottage about seven or so Saturday evening."

Ted was going to play his "hunch."

Saturday at 4:55, the small bell on the gun shop door announced Ted's arrival. He deliberately waited until he was absolutely sure there was no one inside, no one other than the proprietor. Bobby Lee was behind the main counter gathering the day's receipts from his cash register in the corner with his back to the door. He was in a hurry to get to St. Joseph's. When he heard the bell he turned toward his customer. "Hello, how can I..." But then he saw it was Ted. "Counselor, what brings you here?"

"Because I figured it out, Bobby Lee."

"Oh? And what would that be? What did you figure out?"

Ted did not answer. He walked back to bolt the door and then he returned to Bobby Lee. The two men were separated only by a twenty-four-inch counter. Ted turned to the rifle prominently displayed in the mount on the center case. He picked it up and looked at Bobby Lee and said, "Never fails." He put the stock against his right shoulder supporting the firearm with his left hand, with his right index finger on the trigger, as if aiming at an imaginary target. He uttered the word "Pow." Then he replaced the weapon in the display mount. "Never fails," he said again.

He slowly reached into his jacket pocket for a new pair of lime green surgical gloves and he put them on. He pointed to the box of same Burk kept on his workbench. Burk turned his head. Ted picked up the rifle once more, pretending to aim again, and then replaced it in the display mount. Burk watched in silence.

Slipping off the gloves, Ted said, "That's how you did it, Bobby Lee. The M24 was spotless. After you cleaned it, you replaced it in this mount right here and then you waited for some poor schmuck to walk in here and pick it up." Holding up the surgical gloves, "From that point forward you never touched it without wearing a pair of these, even when you took the gun to Cleveland and squeezed off the round. That's how there was only one set of prints on the gun."

Ted threw the surgical gloves down on the display case in front of Bobby Lee. "And the poor schmuck happened to be Tony Icovatti."

Silence.

"Tell me I'm wrong."

Silence.

Calmly, "There was no break-in, Bobby Lee. That was all you. Tell me I'm wrong."

Bobby Lee learned about Icovatti's fingerprints being on the murder weapon just like everyone else learned about it—from reading the newspaper accounts of the assassination. By that time, it was too late. By then, he only had two options: come forward and admit to the crime… or keep quiet and let Icovatti hang. He wasn't going to share with Ted the agony over his decision to remain silent because nothing had changed. If Bobby Lee came forward now, he would go down for the murder of Alexander Chastain and…he would never see Carrie again. He turned to the workbench and picked up a customer's 45-caliber handgun he had just finished cleaning. While staring at Ted and never looking down, he snapped in the clip and laid the handgun down on top of the latex gloves. Ted was in deep trouble. Burk leaned forward and rested both hands on the counter on either side of the handgun.

"So how you gonna' prove all that, Counselor?"

Ted tried to answer without fear in his voice—unsuccessfully. "Won't have to."

"Oh? And why is that?"

"Because you're going to admit to it, Bobby Lee."

"That so? How you figure?"

"Because you want everyone to know you got even, Bobby Lee. The media have turned Chastain into some kind of martyr. You want everyone to know the truth about the real Chastain, the one who violated Carrie. You want to tell the world the real reason Chastain died."

At this, Bobby Lee's eyes started to cloud. He fingered the 45 with Ted watching intensely. "How did you know about Carrie?"

Ted's suspicions were confirmed; he had figured it out. "She told Icovatti...at St. Joseph's. His room was right next to hers."

Burk's thoughts turned to the newspaper left at Carrie's side.

"Chastain and the rest of those guys...are bastards," Ted said. "They're dirty bastards and you're goin' after them, aren't you Bobby Lee?"

"Don't know who they all are yet."

"Let the law do it, Bobby Lee."

"Let the law do it? Are you shittin' me? Look...those fucking bastards deserve to die! Just like Chastain! They fucked my wife...like she was some kind of dog! They killed her! She's dead! Her mind is gone! They fucked her like a dog!" He started to cry. He picked up the 45 and slammed it down so hard it shattered the glass top of the display case. Shards went flying, some hitting Ted, who had turned his head at the last second. Bobby Lee's hand began to bleed.

Ted almost pissed himself. He didn't understand how the goddamn gun didn't go off. He was sweating beads and his heart was racing.

"Bobby Lee, look, I can help you. I can help you nail them. But you have to come forward. You can't let Icovatti go down for this. I promise you we'll get the bastards convicted and then we'll take everything they own...for Carrie...to take care of Carrie."

"Why should I trust you?"

"Because I can get the law to help you."

"Help me? I'll have to do time. Carrie will be left with no one."

"Not like you think. The law's not blind. It accounts for situations like you were in, Bobby Lee. Jesus Christ, they raped your wife!"

"How does it happen?" Bobby Lee was wrapping his hand with the shop rag.

"You're back on the stand on Tuesday. All you need to do is tell the truth. I'll help you through it. They'll take you into custody, but we'll ask the court for a bail hearing the very next day. Bobby Lee... it's the right thing to do. We can't get any help for Carrie if you take them out on your own."

"You sound pretty sure of things."

"I am."

"I'm not committin' to anything. We'll see on Tuesday." His voice was breaking up.

"Okay, Bobby Lee...we'll see on Tuesday." Ted knew not to push.

The bell jingled as Ted unlocked and opened the door to leave. He looked back at Bobby Lee, again all alone, hand bleeding through the rag, tears running down his cheeks, standing over a countertop that was in pieces...shattered, just like his life.

A Weekend at the Cottage

Ted didn't check his messages until after he arrived at the cottage. The first one had been left by his office Friday while he was still in court: "Mr. Chase, we just received a message from some woman who wants to meet with you to discuss the Icovatti prosecution. Since the trial started, the office has been receiving a lot of calls but there was something about this one...we just thought you should hear it for yourself. Let us know if there is anything you need."

"Mr. Chase, I need to speak with you as soon as possible about the Icovatti case. I have some information you need to have. I'll be at your office on Monday. Should be there about noon. Please meet me at your office."

Ted had no clue who the woman was or what she may know, but he did appreciate urgency when he heard it and this sounded urgent. He also sensed a measure of authority. It sounded like she was accustomed to telling others what to do. However, the last thing Ted needed at this point in the trial was to be wasting valuable time chasing down tips.

Ted tossed until he just gave up—sleep was not arriving anytime soon. It was 2:15 Sunday morning when he shuffled out to the cottage's great room, being careful not to bump into anything and wake Dorie. Embers lingered in the wood burner, so he grabbed a small log from the wood box and quietly set it in. He left the heater's hatch slightly open to invite in more air and because the latch squeaked. He sat down in the worn leather chair with his feet on the ottoman and covered his legs with his mother-in-law's afghan, awaiting the rebirth of the fire. After some crackling and popping, the new fire took on the appearance of a battle of canons in the night. The right side of the pine log flared, illuminating the dark room for a nanosecond, then the left side "returned fire"...flash...flash...flash. The artillery encounter was followed by a cavalry charge as the opposing flames rushed toward each other along the log's underside. But there must have been a truce because the adversaries became one at the center, curling around the log's underbelly like the claws of a bird of prey ensnaring its quarry. The wedge of wood rocked forward as if trying to escape its fate but it was devoured from both sides.

Ted was nearing the end of an incredibly difficult trial playing out before the world. He knew his client was not guilty, but he had no idea what Burk would or would not do come Tuesday. The smallest uncertainty in the defense of any criminal matter spelled doom, and here he was with nothing but uncertainty, and some unknown caller had just made it exponentially worse. Ted knew Bobby Lee Burk murdered Alexander Chastain. He knew Tony Icovatti did not. Who in hell was this woman and what did she know? He reached for his cell to listen to her message once again and was surprised to learn there was another:

"Mr. Chase, I have no doubt you have received many prank calls about your case but this is not one of them. I will be at your office Monday about noon."

She was right; his office had received many calls, also e-mails and letters regarding his defense of Corporal Icovatti, but certainly no one came to see him...and without first making arrangements. She had no guarantee Ted would even speak with her, yet here she was directing him to a meeting. And the tone of her voice...she certainly sounded like someone accustomed to giving direction. Ted thought she either had to be nuts and would not show up or...he really didn't know what to think. But he was defending a man that public opinion had already convicted for a murder he did not commit and Ted could not take any chances. He could not leave this stone unturned. He would be in his office on Monday.

The Sunday Morning Roundtable

Nelson: Folks, this morning we are welcoming back Terri Breckenridge from *The Times*, as well as New York criminal defense lawyer, Michael Muelheim. Welcome to you both and it is good to have you back.

Breckenridge: Good to be with you.

Muelheim: Yes, good to be back.

Nelson: Well, what a couple of weeks it has been in Cleveland! The better part of a week to select a jury! High courtroom drama! Many new revelations! And a bomb scare thrown in for good measure! Terri, what do you make of all this?

Breckenridge: What would you have me say...our criminal justice system at work? I think a book or two is in order. (Chuckle)

Nelson: Michael? What do you think of Mr. Chase now?

Muelheim: Carson, by my count, Chase is ahead on points.

Nelson: Really?

Muelheim: Yes. Keep in mind he does not have to prove anything. All he needs to do is interject enough doubt into the State's case so the jury will not reach the standard of proof beyond a reasonable doubt. It appears to me he is very close. Darmstadt didn't hurt him in the least. He got admissions out of the FBI agent and, truth be told, he sliced and diced Dr. Hickman up pretty good. Not bad for a small-town lawyer.

Nelson: Terri, what do you make of Icovatti's court appearance?

Breckenridge: Shocking is all that I would say. Huge sympathy factor coming into play now. Don't see how the jury can ever forget that impression.

Nelson: Michael, Not Guilty or Not Guilty by Reason of Insanity...which way is the defense going here? I honestly can't tell.

Muelheim: Carson, this may be the first case I've seen where alternate theories are being successfully pursued at the same time. As I said, on the fact witnesses, Chase has injected some measure of doubt. On the NGRI, the jury has to buy Hickman...not sure they can do that now. A lot will depend on Chase's expert.

Nelson: Berringer.

Muelheim: That's right. Chase has it set up. He already has the jury thinking Berringer is the guy, the one who really knows Icovatti. The jury buys Berringer, and Chase walks away with a NGRI. Gerrity's got his work cut out for him.

Nelson: Mike, if you were representing Icovatti, which way would you go?

Muelheim: Carson, if Berringer is any good at all, I'd go the insanity route.

Nelson: Why?

Muelheim: It's the safest course. As Terri said, sympathy is coming up big now; the sympathy factor just may be what pushes it over. It would almost be like a compromise verdict.

Nelson: Terri, what about the bomb scare? Any effect?

Breckenridge: Carson, after 9/11, our nation has become more vigilant, but, at the same time, more hardened. When we were kids growing up, there never was such a thing. Now, we see it routinely. Can hardly open a paper without some report somewhere: schools, sporting events, federal buildings, and now a county courthouse. To be honest, by the time the trial reconvenes, I don't think the jury will give it much thought. Not sure it will have any effect at all.

Nelson: Mike?

Muelheim: Agree. No real effect on the court proceedings.

Nelson: Mike, give us your thoughts on Delsander.

Muelheim: He moves it along. Rulings are clear. Frankly, he is doing a fine job...especially considering the events of last Friday.

The discussion of the trial took up the whole hour.

Ted's Dilemma

Before his meeting with the unknown woman, Ted found himself in a place he had never been before. He was literally hours before opening the defense in what the media had dubbed "The Trial of the Decade"... and he had no idea what he was going to do. Panic was setting in. At the outset of the proceedings, the government seemingly had Tony "dead to rights" on the evidence, but Ted believed he had interjected some degree of doubt...and after their expert testified and the jury observed Tony's brief courtroom appearance, Ted grew more confident in a NGRI finding. But where would that leave Tony? With that result, the court retained the power to confine Tony to a mental institution which period of confinement could possibly last for the remainder of his life. Given what Ted knew about Bobby Lee Burk, Tony's confinement to an institution for ANY amount of time was an unjust result; he had committed no crime. Burk was the murderer but Ted understood the justification for his act and, more importantly, Ted agreed with it. He thought of his sister and his father, two people who never recovered from the same vile desecration. The son-of-a-bitch Chastain and his cronies deserved to be punished for what they did. No one, including Bobby Lee Burk or Ted Chase, fully understood Carrie's true role in any of it.

His meeting with Marie Patronite would last for more than four hours. Marie discussed her background and explained what she did for a living; she knew she had to gain his trust before sharing her information. After all, how do you convince someone the Vice President of the United States is a murderer...especially someone you had never met before? Ted was impressed with her appearance, professional manner, and candor. At the same time, he was trying to discern whether she had a hidden agenda.

When Marie felt comfortable and had gained some degree of trust, she began the story about her most recent visit to the Vice President's residence. As soon as she mentioned the Vice President, Ted's radar went up. And when she revealed to Ted she knew for a fact Harley Daull had hired an assassin to take out Chastain, Ted's mind checked out—he was gone, no longer there. His thoughts returned to his sister and his dead father.

Harley Daull! My God, Harley Fucking Daull! The fucking prick from Eau Clair, Wisconsin! How many lives has the bastard ruined?

Patronite pointed out Futrell in the picture of Icovatti's arrest, with Futrell right there looking on. But Marie found she was talking to a zombie with glazed over eyes.

"Mr. Chase? Mr. Chase?" *What the hell was wrong with this guy?*

Ted stood up. "Excuse me."

Given Ted's demeanor, Patronite was apprehensive and she could not conceal it.

"I'm sorry," Ted said. "I need to take a break for a moment. I'll be right back."

He went to the bathroom to throw some cold water on his face. He hadn't been ready for the rage...after so many years

Marie was very worried—for herself, not for Ted. *Does he not understand I'll be hung out to dry if this does not go well?*

When he returned five minutes later, she asked seriously, "You okay?"

"Yes. Fine. Sorry."

A thousand questions followed. Ted needed to know every detail about Daull and how she knew what she knew. She showed him the newspaper with Rhuloc Futrell standing next to Tony Icovatti as he was being arrested by the FBI agents. Her accusations against a sitting

Vice President could not be more serious...or actionable, should they be found not credible. Everything she had, indeed everything she had become, was at stake here. She needed to satisfy herself Ted could carry the load…and he ensured her of that in the remainder of the interview.

After their meeting, Ted was confident Marie was telling the truth about what she knew.

Juries in criminal cases look for credibility and consistency from the defense Mac had taught Ted, and those concepts were related. Presenting two alternative theories—Not Guilty and Not Guilty by Reason of Insanity was very risky. Given the proceedings thus far, the NGRI path was probably Ted's best option to save his client's life. But Burk had confirmed for Ted such a finding would be the wrong result: Tony Icovatti was innocent. And now, there was Patronite.

Let's say Burk does deliver a confession on the witness stand. Should Ted just completely throw away the NGRI?

And Ted had no assurance Burk was going to come forward at the eleventh hour. On the other hand, Patronite, in an incredibly convincing manner, was sure the Vice President of the United States was responsible for this murder. Ted was confident she would be very convincing should she be called to the stand. Compared to Burk, Patronite was a sure thing. After all, she just traveled half-way across the country at her own expense to carry it through.

After Ted dropped Patronite at her hotel, his mind was racing. Should he stick with the NGRI defense and try to get Tony out as soon as possible? Or put Burk on the stand and let him go down...if he told the truth…a huge "if."

His thoughts drifted to his sister...and his dead father.

Tuesday, Back in the Box

There was a different Bobby Lee waiting to enter the witness box. His Friday look of confidence, even arrogance, while on the stand was now gone. His head was down, his eyes red and swollen, one hand bandaged. When he did look up, his eyes darted around the courtroom but never toward Ted, who was watching his every move. He avoided any acknowledgment of Ted while he waited for Judge Delsander to take control of his room, get the proceedings underway, and call him back to the stand. He knew he was going away but he did not fear it nor did he feel any shame in it. Chastain deserved death and Bobby Lee delivered it to him. What he did fear was the possibility he would not be returning…until it was too late for Carrie. It was this fear that was now in control of him and he could not hide it.

Even before the judge took the bench, Delsander's bailiff directed Bobby Lee to the stand. He was now closer to the jury, head down, reddened eyes watering so much he needed a handkerchief to keep his cheeks dry. Juror Number 3, the emergency room nurse, commented to Number 4, "He looks like he hasn't slept in days." Everyone in the courtroom was perplexed. *What happened to this man? He was just a shop owner who had a rifle stolen. Why is he so upset?*

When Delsander took the bench, his bailiff nodded toward Burk and the judge glanced at him...and was confused. Even before he brought the room to order, he addressed Bobby Lee.

"Mr. Burk, are you alright?"

"Yes, Your Honor."

"Do you need some time before we start?"

"No, Your Honor. I just want to get this over with."

"It appears something is bothering you."

"No...I'm sorry. I'll be fine."

Ted was listening closely to the exchange.

"Very well then." One loud clap of the gavel. "The court will come to order. Mr. Burk, just a reminder that you are still under oath. Mr. Chase, your witness."

The biggest gamble of Ted's entire life lay before him. If he passed on Burk, he was putting all Tony's eggs in one basket, held by Patronite...and there was no guarantee of the outcome.

Everything he had learned about trial practice told him not to do it. He had to fight hard to keep his poker face and not reveal the slightest trace of indecision to the jury. He slid his chair back and stood but did not come out from behind counsel table. Bobby Lee still refused to look him in the face.

Ted slowly said, "I have no questions for this witness." *There...the die is cast; the Rubicon has been crossed.*

At first, Bobby Lee was unsure what he had heard. He looked up with a puzzled expression on his face and then he heard Judge Delsander, "Very well then. Mr. Burk, you may step down."

"I'm done?"

"Yes, Mr. Chase has no questions for you. You are free to go."

"I don't understand."

"Your testimony is over. Am I right, Mr. Chase?"

"Yes, Your Honor. No questions."

"You are free to go, Mr. Burk."

Bobby Lee was confused. *What was going on? How can I be free to go? Is Chase going to let Icovatti go down? That can't be it. What the hell is going on?* He slowly rose from the witness chair and glanced up at Ted who was still on his feet but no longer acknowledging him, even when Burk walked right past him to retake his first-row seat. Ted was scared to death and trying his hardest not to let it show.

After Gerrity rested his case, Delsander addressed the jury, "Ladies and gentlemen, at the outset of the trial, the defense elected to defer their opening statement to the beginning of their case, which is their option. We are now there. Mr. Chase, you have the floor."

Ted rose slowly but made no effort to reach the podium. "Your Honor, the defense waives their opening." Another curveball at Gerrity who was now totally confused. What in the hell was this guy doing?

Judge Delsander appeared confused as well, "I'm sorry?"

"The defense does not wish to make a statement to the jury but wishes to go right to the presentation of its evidence."

Very slowly, glaring at Ted, "Alright...very well then I guess... please call your first witness." *Is this guy trying to create an issue for the Court of Appeals?*

"Your Honor, the defense calls Marie Patronite." *And fuck you forever, Daull...*

The rear doors to the courtroom opened and a young, attractive woman with flowing blond hair immediately commanded everyone's attention. She was carrying a folded newspaper in her left hand. Her step was certain and her manner confident. But who the hell was she and why was she here?

She took the oath.

Ted began, "Ms. Patronite, I understand you live in New York City, is that correct?"

"Yes."

"And what is it that you do for a living?"

"Political research."

"Can you explain that for us? What exactly does a political researcher do?"

"I am retained by a candidate for public office or his political party to investigate opponents."

"Someone running for political office hires you to explore the background of the person he or she is running against."

"That's right."

A murmur in the courtroom.

Ted paused to let it pass..."What is it that you look for?"

"Information that would be useful to my client's campaign."

The courtroom began to stir, like a large animal slowly awakening from its nap.

At this answer, Ted turned ever so slightly so he could steal a glance at the jury panel. He knew everyone in the courtroom just translated her last statement to mean she was a person who was paid to dig up dirt. He held no doubt the answer would, right off the bat, lessen rather than enhance her stock with the jury. But now, more than any other witness in this trial, he needed the jury to buy into everything Marie Patronite was about to say...and it appeared he was getting off on the wrong foot. He also recognized that his credibility with the jury, which he had worked so very hard to establish from day one of the trial was now on the line. He had just made the biggest roll of the dice in his entire life...with the fate of another human being in the balance. Ted's bet was that the jury's initial disapproval of his star witness would be fleeting, replaced with their confidence in the truth of the testimony to follow. If he lost the bet, he...and Tony Icovatti...would come up "craps."

Every person in the spectator seats and jury box was even more alert, if that were possible. *Where the hell was all this going? Is it possible the case of the murder of a U.S. senator can somehow be bigger than it already is?*

Ted hoped so—he was orchestrating its growth.

He waited about a ten count. Silence in the courtroom, not noise, gets everyone's attention. He very slowly asked, "Can you share with the jury who your latest client was?"

"Certainly," Patronite replied, just as slowly, but very calculated, "Vice President Harley Daull."

The animal began to roar and the gaveling started and it did not stop for several minutes. The jury and attendees now realized this witness operated on the national stage.

Now I've got them, Ted thought.

"Ladies and gentlemen, please understand you are here only as guests of the Court. Please do not jeopardize your invitation." Judge Delsander made his point and silence returned to the courtroom.

Ted slowed down even more. He wanted everyone in the room to say to themselves, *Hurry up. Don't leave us hanging. Ask the goddamn next question already.*

At a snail's pace and in a measured tone Ted asked, "And who did the Vice President retain you to research?"

"Senator Alexander Chastain."

The animal roared louder and longer this time.

"Ladies and gentlemen, this courtroom will be cleared if this testimony is interrupted again. Sheriff, please bring in the deputies you have outside the door." Delsander was growing impatient with the interruptions. An uneasy silence returned.

"How much were you paid for your services?"

"Twenty-five thousand dollars." Patronite deliberately left out the part about not being paid the balance of her fee; she did not want to appear before the jury as having an "agenda" and...no one in the courtroom could possibly be the wiser.

"Was your research successful?"

"Very."

Stirring from the back of the courtroom...drawing a stern look in that direction from the bench. Burk bristled. His knuckles were white, grasping the edge of his wooden pew.

"I see. And you have been following this trial in the media?"

"Yes."

"Newspaper, television?"

"Yes, both. And online."

"And you contacted my office toward the end of last week, is that true?"

"Yes."

"And why did you do that?"

"Because I had information about this matter you and these folks here need to know." She was pointing at the jury with one hand and with her other clenching the newspaper in her lap.

Bobby Lee Burk's eyes were boring holes through her body. He was having trouble breathing. So was Ted but he didn't let it show.

"And that's why you travelled here this weekend and asked me to put you on the stand?"

"Yes."

Ted stopped...dead still. He very slowly walked back to counsel table while glancing at his opponent, who, like everyone else in the room, could not wait to hear his next question. Very deliberately...Ted reached for the pitcher of water on the table while looking down at Mac who hid his wry smile from everyone in the room except Ted.

His student had learned well and was now the master. Silence, not noise, gets everyone's attention.

Ted poured a small glass of water and took a sip. Unknowingly, he reminded almost everyone in the courtroom of the now-famous images of Chastain just before the back of his head exploded. Still with his back to Patronite, facing the spectators in the courtroom and looking out over them, he loudly asked, "And what is it that we all need to know?"

Swallowing hard....Patronite waited a minute to gather her wits. She needed to sound as convincing as possible. "You need to know that Corporal Icovatti did not kill Alexander Chastain."

The gavel immediately started in a futile attempt to calm the courtroom down. To Burk, it seemed Delsander pounded forever. No admonition this time. The judge was having a hard time himself with the tension. Silence eventually returned.

Another long pause...still looking out over the spectators rather than at the witness, Ted asked loudly: "And how do you know that?"

Lifting up *The New York Times* she had clenched in her hand, she pointed to the picture of Tony in Cleveland being surrounded by the FBI agents after the fatal shot, the picture that had made its way to the front page of almost every newspaper in the world, the picture with Rhuloc Futrell standing right beside Tony. *Screw you, Daull*, she thought to herself. She pointed to Futrell and said, "Because I know for a fact that Vice President Harley Daull paid this man right here one hundred thousand dollars to kill Senator Chastain. His name is Rhuloc Futrell."

The courtroom erupted.

Patronite was on the stand for two hours.

Ted's only wish was that his sister and father could be there with him.

The Cottage

It was growing late. Dorie had been asleep for hours. Ted was sitting in his favorite worn leather chair with his feet on the ottoman, staring at the wood burner. As the orange-black embers were slowly dying, the small room was growing dark. The fading rumble of the thunder told him the evening storm had passed. In his lap was the Bible, opened to the Gospel of Matthew and the Sermon on the Mount. In a whisper, he read to himself: "Blessed are the peacemakers for they shall be called the children of God."

The jury acquitted Tony Icovatti but they were powerless to free him from his personal demons. Chester Mylott cut a deal and turned on Daull. Both plead guilty to conspiracy to commit murder and were in custody. Rhuloc Futrell disappeared with his hundred thousand and was never heard from again. Bobby Lee Burk got a "walk" courtesy of Ted and would commence Carrie's lawsuit against Chastain's estate the following month.

Was Alexander Chastain a peacemaker? Perhaps...in his own twisted way. And Sally Colonna? His family certainly believed so. What about Tony Icovatti? Probably. Chastain was dead and Sally was literally blown to bits. He died without purpose on worthless sand along with 4,500 of his countrymen. And Tony? He was only half a man, trapped within an eternal darkness...never to escape. The war had ended but the world was the same. Nothing had changed... except for thousands of families left in ruin.

Forsaken are the peacemakers.